A Children's Encyclopedia of
HORSES & PONIES

Written by
Christopher Rawson, Joanna Spector
and Elizabeth Polling

Illustrated by
Eric Rowe, Fred'k. St. Ward
Gordon King, Joan Thompson
and Rhoda Burns

Designed by
Bob Scott

Consultant and contributor
Patricia Smyly

The material in this book from pages 2–31,
and from pages 34–63 is also available as
separate titles: *Inside the World of Horses*
and *A Practical Guide to Riding & Pony Care*,
published by Usborne Publishing Ltd.

Printed in Belgium by Henri Proost, Turnhout, Belgium.

First published in 1978   Published in Australia   Published in Canada by
Usborne Publishing Ltd   by Rigby Ltd   Hayes Publishing Ltd,
20 Garrick Street,   Adelaide, Sydney, Perth,   Burlington, Ontario
London WC2E 9BJ   Melbourne, Brisbane.

A Children's Encyclopedia of HORSES & PONIES

Contents

How Horses Began

The world of horses is a very exciting and interesting one. Although most working horses have now been replaced by cars, lorries and tractors, there are many different horse sports and still some jobs that only horses can do.

Horses are gentle, friendly animals. They are easy to teach if their training is done with patience, experience and lots of time. As well as being used for riding, horses are bred and trained as race horses, hunters and carriage horses. They are also taught to do difficult dressage movements, to be expert show jumpers, and to take part in displays.

Horses and ponies have a very long history. There were herds of horses roaming the world long before the first people, who lived about a million years ago. At that time horses looked quite different from modern ones.

At first men hunted the wild horses which lived in Asia and Europe for food. Later people began to use them to carry goods, food and weapons, and to ride them. Over the centuries, horses and ponies changed men's way of life. People could travel much farther and faster on horseback or in carts than on foot. Mounted warriors could easily defeat enemies on foot and farmers could grow bigger crops with horse-drawn ploughs and farm machinery. With careful selection and breeding for different jobs and sports, these useful animals have become the horses we know today.

Eohippus (The Dawn Horse)

The first pre-historic animals to be recognized as horses were timid little creatures. They lived in the woodlands of North America and Europe about 55 million years ago. They were about the size of a fox but looked like a small deer. Their colouring helped them to hide among the trees from large meat-eating animals. They could not bite off grass with their teeth so they lived on soft leaves and young plants. They had four toes on each front foot and three on each of their hind feet. Each toe had a small round hoof at the end. This was the main clue to the discovery that Eohippus was the first horse.

Mesohippus

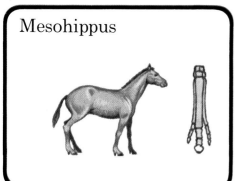

After about 20 million years the Dawn horses had changed to look like this. They had grown a little taller and had three toes on each foot. They lived more in the open, ate grass, and could run faster.

Merychippus

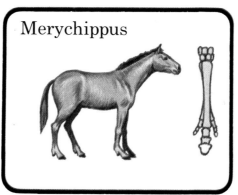

After millions of years, horses had become about 1 metre taller and lived on the open plains. They still had three toes on each foot but the centre one had grown larger and the side ones were smaller.

Pliohippus

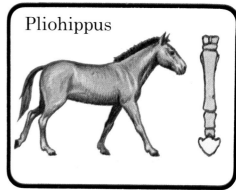

The first true one-toed horses lived about five million years ago. By then they looked much more like modern horses. Pliohippus was also the ancient ancestor of the zebras and asses of today.

Domestication

Primitive men in Europe hunted horses for food for thousands of years. About 4,000 years ago, they began to capture them instead of killing them. The first people to tame horses were probably the tribesmen who roamed the treeless plains of Central Asia. They kept small herds of the tough little ponies which lived there for their meat, milk and skins. These people learned to harness the ponies so they could pull loads and they also began to ride them.

Southern Horse

Two quite different types of horses developed in Europe and Asia. In Southern Europe they became fine-boned with smooth coats. They could run very fast and were like Arab horses of today.

Northern Horse

Only much tougher ponies could live in the cooler weather of Northern Asia. They had thick skins and long, rough coats. They probably looked like this Przvalski, or wild Mongolian, horse.

Some Famous Breeds

There are now nearly 200 official breeds of horses and ponies in the world. They all came from the Northern or Southern types. Different breeds developed over millions of years, due to changes in the weather and the food where they lived. Horses that did not adapt to these changes died out. Only small, hardy ponies could survive in the cold, mountainous areas of Northern Europe. Larger, heavier types of horses lived in the warm, grassy lowlands. Light-boned, fast animals developed in the hot, dry regions of Southern Asia. Many years of careful matching and cross-breeding produced the horses we know today. On these pages are some of the horses that have been bred for a particular job or sport.

German Riding and Carriage Horses

Most of the German breeds, such as the Hanoverian shown here, were the result of crossing heavy Northern horses with fine English Thoroughbreds. One of the most popular breeds, the Trakhener, was bred from an English Thoroughbred, Perfectionist. These horses were used mainly for pulling carriages. Now they have become lighter and more elegant in build and are very good at dressage, show jumping and eventing. Another German breed, the Oldenberg, has become famous for driving events.

East European Horses

In Poland and Hungary horses developed in much the same way as in Germany but with more Arab horses used for cross-breeding. The Soviet Union has the biggest variety of horses because there are so many different types of country and weather inside its borders. Its ponies are very tough and hardy and are able to live on very little food. Many Russian horses are bred for trotting races, like this Akhal Teke horse.

American Horses

All the North American breeds were developed from European horses taken across the Atlantic by early settlers. The Tennessee Walking Horse, shown here, was used by farmers in the South. Their special running walk gave a smooth ride. The lively Criollo ponies of South America, used for herding cattle, developed from the horses brought by the Spanish who invaded Mexico in the 16th century.

Southern European Horses

Very attractive and popular types of horses live in Southern Europe. They usually have short legs, deep bodies and grey coats. They include the Andalusian horses of Spain and Portugal, shown here, the famous Lipizzaners, and the Camargue ponies of Southern France. They are all closely related to the old Barb horses which were probably brought to Spain by Arab invaders. These horses are especially good at the high-school work which became fashionable in Vienna in the 17th century and has been carried on ever since.

English Thoroughbreds

These noble horses are the result of cross-breeding native British ponies of the Northern type with Barb, Turk and Arabian horses of the Southern type. The Thoroughbred has been developed into a perfect racing animal. It is also an excellent riding horse with good proportions and natural balance. They make good hunters and jumpers when crossed with part-Thoroughbred or part-Arab horses.

Heavy Horses

The mild weather and lush grass in France, Holland and Germany helped to develop the heavy horses. They are a much larger and stronger type of the Northern horse and were produced by carefully breeding the largest animals. They were once war horses and used as chargers by French knights. Modern French breeds include the Percheron and Breton. In Britain heavy horses like these Shire horses were used for all farm work. Other breeds such as Suffolk Punches and Clydesdales are still very popular.

Horse Transport

Horses have been used to pull wagons and carriages for thousands of years. One of the oldest ever found was the state chariot of Egypt's boy king, Tutankhamen, who lived over 3,000 years ago. Until the beginning of this century, when motor cars took over, the only way to travel fast or move heavy loads overland was to use horses.

Coaching

The mail and passenger coaches in the 18th century were the fastest and most comfortable ever built. They were better made than other wagons and carriages and their improved suspension gave travellers a smoother ride. There were good stopping places about every 24km along the coach roads, where the teams of four horses were changed. The tired horses were left there and fresh ones pulled the coaches to the next stopping place. Coach horses were chosen for their speed and strength. But the work was so hard that coach horses could rarely be used for more than about three years. Coaches like this carried passengers all over Europe.

Coaching

Chariot

Greek war chariots, like this one, were used in battle until about 700 BC. After that, they were used for hunting and chariot races. These were exciting but dangerous.

Farm Cart

This type of farm wagon was used from the 14th century onwards. It could be pulled by several horses in a line. The traces and much of the harness were made of rope.

European Chaise

Fashionable and rich gentlemen took up driving as a sport late in the 18th century. They drove this type of light two-wheeled cart in towns and on their country estates.

Parts of a Harness

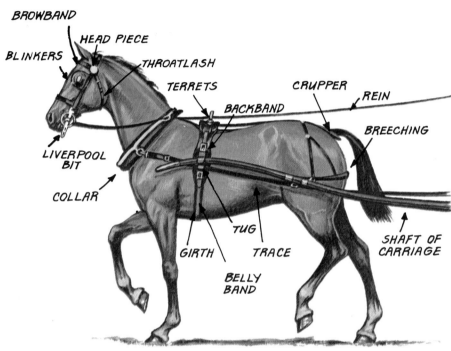

BROWBAND

HEAD PIECE

BLINKERS

THROATLASH

TERRETS

CRUPPER

REIN

BACKBAND

BREECHING

LIVERPOOL BIT

COLLAR

TUG

SHAFT OF CARRIAGE

GIRTH

TRACE

BELLY BAND

Driving harness may look complicated, but each part is carefully made to let the horse pull comfortably and give the driver maximum control. Most important is the collar, which should fit perfectly, and the traces, with which the horse pulls the vehicle. Tugs on the backband support the shafts which stop the vehicle from tipping. The breeching fits round the hindquarters and is attached to the shafts or the traces to hold the vehicle back on steep hills or when slowing down.

Covered Wagon

Settlers travelling to the West of America had carts, called Prairie Schooners, like this one. They were pulled by horses or oxen and carried all the family possessions.

Charabanc

This is what a coach party looked like about a hundred years ago. The vehicle was called a charabanc and was used on large country estates to carry members of shooting parties, or the servants and guns. Later charabancs were used for public sight-seeing tours.

War Horses

Horses have probably been used in war since men first learned to ride them. The Assyrians had mounted bowmen in about 900 BC. They must have trained their horses well because the bowmen needed both hands to shoot. Since then and until the beginning of the 20th century, mounted soldiers have been an important part of armies. Horses were also used to carry baggage, food and weapons, and to pull cannons and heavy guns.

1 Romans

The Roman cavalry, who wore metal armour, needed strong horses to carry the extra weight. A special breed was developed for them. The Romans did not have saddles or stirrups so they had to grip their horses with their thighs and could carry only light weapons. They were armed with a spear, a shield and a short sword.

2 Tartars

These fierce horsemen, led by Ghenghis Khan, conquered land from the China Sea to the Baltic Sea in the 13th century. They could travel up to 128 km a day on their tough Mongolian ponies. The Tartars even ate and slept on horseback. They were the first to use snaffle bridles, and saddles with stirrups.

3 Knights of the Middle Ages

These soldiers rode into battle on huge horses, called destriers. By the 13th century both the men and their horses had become too heavily armoured. Slow and clumsy, they were easily defeated by bowmen in such battles as Crecy and Agincourt between the French and English.

8

4 Cavalry Regiments

Cavalry again became the strongest attacking force in most armies in the 17th, 18th and 19th centuries. Many of the great battles in Europe were won by famous cavalry commanders, such as Charles II of Sweden, Frederick the Great of Prussia, Napoleon of France and Marlborough and Wellington of England.

Frederick the Great was the first commander to understand the importance of good feed and proper training for cavalry horses. He also provided extra horses, called remounts, for soldiers whose horses were killed or injured in action. He introduced horse artillery to the battlefield. Six horses, in pairs, pulled the heavy fields guns. These were fired at the enemy before the cavalry charged them.

Here the British and French cavalry are in action at the Battle of Waterloo in 1815. French soldiers charged at the trot while the British galloped into battle.

The two most famous chargers at this time were Napoleon's grey Arab stallion, called Marengo, and Wellington's chestnut stallion, called Copenhagen.

5 The 20th Century

By the beginning of the First World War, which started in 1914, machine guns which could fire up to 800 bullets a minute, field guns which fired high-explosive shells, and quick-firing rifles had all been invented. Horses could not be protected from these weapons and the cavalry were often replaced by tanks and armoured cars. The last big cavalry charge was at Musino, near Moscow, during the Second World War. In ten minutes, 2,000 Russian mounted soldiers were killed by German guns.

Cavalry is no longer used by armies today but most countries still have some mounted soldiers for state and official ceremonies.

9

Working Horses

When men began to farm instead of only hunting for food many thousands of years ago, they first found a use for horses instead of just killing them to eat. Until the middle of the 19th century, horses still did much of the heavy work for farmers and pulled many different sorts of carts and wagons. Some are still used today for work that machines cannot do. Here are some of the jobs that horses did in the past and still do.

19th Century

One of the most exciting jobs for horses was pulling the heavy, steam fire engines in the 19th century. This American 'steamer' is rushing to a fire at full gallop. The man at the back of the engine is the 'stoker'. He is trying to get up enough steam to work the powerful water pumps as soon as they reach the fire. These horses were especially selected for their speed and strength.

Draught Horses

Heavy draught horses, such as the Percheron, Jutland or these Shire horses, were first bred to carry knights in armour into battle. They were so strong, they were soon being used to pull the ploughs on farms and heavy barges on the canals. They were also used on roads to draw heavy loads, such as timber and coal. Most of this work is now done by powerful lorries but heavy horses are still kept by some breweries to deliver beer in the city centres.

These horses are pulling a beer dray. It is a low, open-sided wagon. The barrels are stacked on top of the dray and sometimes also slung underneath.

Shrimp Fishers

This unusual type of work for horses can be seen on the Belgian coast. Placid and solidly-built Breton horses drag trawl nets through the shallow water to catch shrimps.

Horses are still very useful in other areas, such as mountains. High in the Austrian Tyrol, pretty chestnut Haflinger ponies pull felled trees over rough ground that is too steep for machines. Hardy Fjord ponies in Scandinavia do the same sort of work.

Ranching

In America, Australia and New Zealand horses are widely used on ranches. Most of their work is herding cattle or sheep from one pasture to another. Some breeds, such as the American Quarterhorse, are trained to 'cut', or single out, one animal from the herd, and help the rider when he ropes it.

Pit Ponies

There were over 70,000 pit ponies working in Britain's coal mines in 1900. Now there are only about 100 left. Tough native breeds, such as Shetland, Welsh and Fell ponies, pulled the tubs of coal on tracks along the narrow passages. They lived underground from the age of about four until too old to work.

11

Famous Show Jumpers in Action

Show jumping looks an exciting way of life if you watch famous riders at a show or on television. But to become a top-class rider needs a lot of hard work and training. Show jumpers have to be totally dedicated and spend most of their lives riding and training their horses. They also have to find and train young horses for the future years. But for the few who do succeed, the rewards are great. Here are some who have become famous through skill and determination.

Hartwig Steenken

This very talented rider is seen here on Kosmos. But most of Steenken's successes were with the Hanoverian mare called Simona. With her he won the 1974 World title and rode in the winning team at the Munich Olympics.

Eddie Macken

One of Ireland's most outstanding young riders, he has won most of the top awards in Europe on Boomerang pictured here. Macken finished second to Hartwig Steenken in the 1974 World Championship, riding Pele.

Harvey Smith

Seen here on the German horse, Salvador, Harvey Smith is one of the great personalities of show jumping. He bought his first horse for £40 and was soon asked to join the British team. He rode in the Mexico and Munich Olympics, and has won five British Grands Prix.

Behind the Scenes

Grooms travel with the horses to show jumping events to look after them. There are wooden stables at most big shows.

Preparing the horses for jumping must be done with great care. This groom is putting on tendon boots to protect the horse's legs.

If the ground is soft or the horse may have to turn sharply, metal studs are screwed into his shoes to stop him slipping.

A rider needs time to get ready before jumping. She must wear the right number. This rider is buckling on her spurs.

Alwin Schockemöhle

This popular German rider won the individual gold medal in the Montreal Olympics in 1976 riding Warwick. He has been German national champion three times and is here riding Rex the Robber.

David Broome

One of Britain's most stylish riders, Broome is able to coax the best out of any horse. Here he is riding Red 'A'. He has won two Olympic bronze medals, the 1970 World title and three European titles.

Rodney Jenkins

The most successful American show jumper, here riding Number One Spy, he has won a huge number of championships. His most famous horse is the gelding, Idle Dice.

Some horses have to be 'warmed-up' in the practice area for a long time. Others need only one or two practice jumps.

All the tack must be checked before the event. This horse is having his bit adjusted and the girth may be tightened.

While waiting for his turn, a rider will walk his horse round. He may keep the rugs on until the last minute if it is cold.

After the horse has jumped, the groom gives him a tit-bit and puts on his rugs. He will loosen the girth and walk the horse until cool.

Great Show Jumping Events

Show jumping is a very expert sport, with valuable prizes to be won at all the important events. But there are still some special competitions, such as the Olympic Games, which all riders hope to win regardless of the prize money. The winners of these sorts of competitions have reached the top of their sport. Riders who earn their living by riding are called professionals. All others are called amateurs.

Olympic Games

The Olympic gold, silver and bronze medals are the most highly valued awards in show jumping. The Games take place every four years. Many riders spend the years in between them preparing their horses. Only amateur riders may take part which means that some well-known professional riders cannot compete. This might make the medals seem easier to win but competition is always keen. Alwin Schockemöhle's winning performance at the Montreal Olympics was outstanding. Here he is riding Warwick Rex. He was the only entrant to jump all the fences twice without a fault. It was one of the most difficult Olympic courses ever built.

Individual Grand Prix Olympic Games 1976

A course builder has to think of many things when he is designing a course. He tries to set the competitors as many different problems as possible. So he builds a course with a variety of jumps, with different turns and distances between them. The course should test the rider by making him work out how to ride it. It tests the horse for obedience, suppleness and jumping ability. This was the course for the first round in the 1976 Olympics.

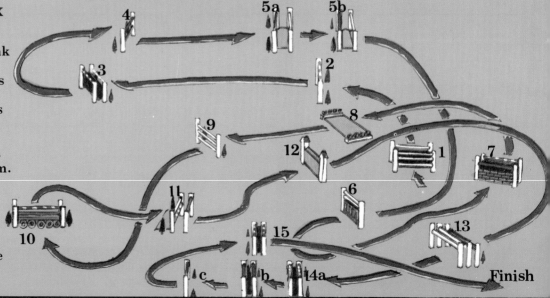

World Championship

This is also held every four years, between the Olympics. It is open to amateur and professional riders. It is usually held in the country of the rider who last won the Championship. This event is a great test of horsemanship because the best four riders have to ride each others horses. This means that the rider with the most difficult horse often wins. Hartwig Steenken on Simona (left) won in 1974.

British Jumping Derby

This event is held at Hickstead in Great Britain every year. It is different from other competitions because natural obstacles, such as banks, hedges and ditches, are included in the course.

It is also very long and difficult. It needs great concentration and strength by horses and riders. One feature of the course is the Derby Bank. Here Judy Crago on Bouncer shows how to

come down the Bank by sliding from the top and jumping off about two-thirds of the way down. They finished equal second in 1976. The winner was Eddie Macken on Boomerang.

European Championships

This is quite a simple type of competition. It usually has two rounds with the scores from each round added together. If any riders then have equal scores, they jump again and the fastest one with the fewest faults wins. The Championship takes place every two years and, until 1973, there were separate ones for men and women. The winner that year was Paddy McMahon of Great Britain on Pennwood Forge Mill (above).

Problem Fences

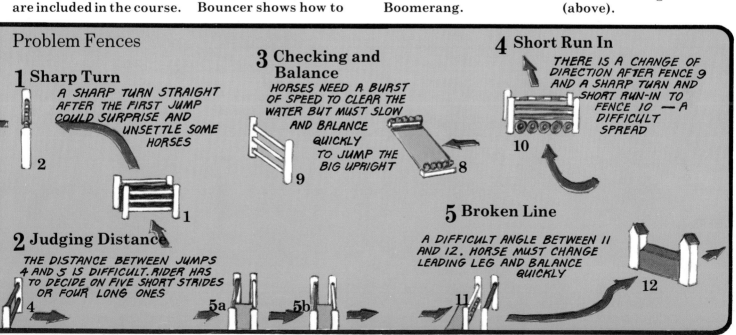

1 Sharp Turn
A SHARP TURN STRAIGHT AFTER THE FIRST JUMP COULD SURPRISE AND UNSETTLE SOME HORSES

2 Judging Distance
THE DISTANCE BETWEEN JUMPS 4 AND 5 IS DIFFICULT. RIDER HAS TO DECIDE ON FIVE SHORT STRIDES OR FOUR LONG ONES

3 Checking and Balance
HORSES NEED A BURST OF SPEED TO CLEAR THE WATER BUT MUST SLOW AND BALANCE QUICKLY TO JUMP THE BIG UPRIGHT

4 Short Run In
THERE IS A CHANGE OF DIRECTION AFTER FENCE 9 AND A SHARP TURN AND SHORT RUN-IN TO FENCE 10 — A DIFFICULT SPREAD

5 Broken Line
A DIFFICULT ANGLE BETWEEN 11 AND 12. HORSE MUST CHANGE LEADING LEG AND BALANCE QUICKLY

Showing

Show classes for horses and ponies are held at most local and international horse shows. Anyone with a suitable horse or pony can take part. The essentials are that a horse has good conformation—that is, a good shape—straight action and 'clean' or undamaged legs. He must also be well-mannered and schooled. There are classes for all types of horses and ponies. Most are ridden but some are 'in hand' or led. Other classes are combined with performance, such as dressage or jumping.

Child's Ridden Pony

Private Driving

Private Driving

Driving for pleasure is becoming a popular hobby. Many shows now hold special driving classes for private 'turnouts'. The pony must be correctly harnessed and the vehicle smartly painted. A judge looks for good action and responses from the pony. The most exciting horses to watch in harness are Hackneys. With their high, graceful stepping action, they seem to float over the ground.

Child's Ridden Pony

These classes are usually divided into three parts; for ponies up to 12.2, 13.2 and 14.2 hands, ridden by children up to 12, 14 and 16 years old. The judge looks for an attractive 'well-made' pony which moves nicely and is well schooled. He must have good manners and be safe, obedient and trustworthy.

Arabs

Arabs

Arab horses are usually shown 'in-hand', or led, with mane and tail flowing, never plaited. There are also ridden and performance classes for them. Points the judges look for include a small head, a short back, sloping shoulders and free but straight leg action. All Arabs must be pure-bred and registered.

Preparing to Show

1 There is lots of hard work to be done before a show. All the tack must be spotlessly clean with the bit and stirrups polished.

2 The final grooming will be done on the morning of the show. This may include washing any white leg markings.

3 Next comes plaiting. This must be done very neatly. Sections of mane are plaited, folded under and sewn into place.

4 Horses sometimes become excited before a class. Twenty minutes on the lunge often helps them relax and warm up quietly.

Cobs

Cobs are small, stocky horses of not more than 15.3 hands, and of no particular breed. They were first bred as riding horses for heavy or elderly riders and must be very well behaved. In cob, hunter and hack classes, the riders dismount to allow the judge to put their horses through their paces himself. The judge may then see the horse unsaddled and have him led to watch his action and overall appearance.

Hunters

Hunters are generally divided into classes by the weight they can carry when hunting. They must be strong, obedient and have a good galloping action.

Hacks

These are elegant riding horses that must have nearly perfect conformation and manners. There are often Ladies Hack classes which are ridden side-saddle.

In the Ring

At the first line-up the best horses come out in turn to give a short, individual show, which the riders plan beforehand.

The judge may then want to look at the horses more closely. The saddles are taken off so he can judge the overall shape.

He will then ask to see each horse trotted up in-hand. He can then tell if the action is straight or there is a fault.

The horses are remounted and the judge makes his final decision. They are called into line for the presentations.

Dressage

Dressage is quite simply the training of a horse for riding. It can be used just to make him more obedient and comfortable to ride, or to get him ready for other things like show jumping. But dressage in its purest form goes a lot further than that. It prepares the horse for exacting tests of obedience and movement. The main object is to show that he can move lightly and freely while carrying a rider and willingly obey commands.

Everything should look natural and easy, with the rider's aids, or signals, almost invisible.

Dressage competitions are held at many levels, from preliminary to advanced, and then there are special classes such as Prix St Georges and Grand Prix. Three judges mark each movement separately and their marks are then added together. Here are some famous dressage horses and riders in action.

Piaffe

This is one of the most difficult movements in an advanced test. It is a slow trot, on the spot. The horse springs from one front leg and opposite hind leg to the other opposite legs as if he were moving forward. It is a test of balance, strength and control.

Reiner Klimke

Dr Reiner Klimke and his horse, Mehmed, were one of West Germany's top dressage partnerships. They won the World championship in 1974 and were bronze medallists at the Montreal Olympics. Here they are making a change of tempo, or pace, from working trot to collected trot. Even small changes in tempo have to be shown clearly and made at exactly the right place. This has to be done without upsetting the horse's balance or rhythm.

Christine Stückelberger

This young rider from Switzerland reached the top of her sport when she won the gold medal at the Montreal Olympics in 1976. Here she is riding Granat, a big German-bred Holstein horse, in Vienna. They are performing a collected trot. Christine started riding at the age of 13 when an aunt paid for some lessons as a present. Since then she has been Swiss champion six times. She is trained by Georg Wahl, a pupil of the Spanish Riding School.

Pirouette

This tests the suppleness of the horse's spine and his balance. He turns a complete circle on the spot in a collected canter. He keeps all four feet moving in the canter sequence. The hind feet step almost in the same spot. The front legs step in a circle round them.

Harry Boldt

Harry Boldt on Woycheck was a runner-up in Montreal for West Germany. Here they are performing a pirouette. The horse's weight is over his inside hind leg.

Tonny Jensen

This is Tonny Jensen of Denmark riding Fox. He is just finishing a series of changes of leg at the canter.

Dominique d'Esme

Dominique d'Esme is one of France's most successful dressage riders. Here she is riding Carioca II in an extended trot. The extended paces are most difficult as the horse must have a very strong back and hindquarters. This pace is not faster than the others but the strides are longer and lower.

Jennie Loriston-Clarke

Jennie Loriston-Clarke is one of Britain's top dressage riders. Here she is competing on Kadett in the Munich Olympic Games. The horse is performing a collected canter down the centre of the arena. In movements like this, the horse has to move in a perfectly straight line, just as a circle must be ridden perfectly round.

19

Eventing

This is one of the hardest and most exciting horse sports. Major events last for three days. They test riders and their horses in three ways. Dressage tests a horse's obedience and control. Cross-country tests his strength, fitness and agility. Show jumping tests that he is still fit and able to jump accurately even when he is tired after the long cross-country part.

The idea for this competition came from the army. Cavalry horses had to be obedient, able to gallop across country, jump anything and work again the next day. Event horses need years of training before they are ready to take part in top class events.

1 Dressage

The dressage test is on the first day. It shows if a horse is obedient to the rider and if the rider is giving the right signals to the horse. The judges look for a supple horse that moves obediently and is calm and has an even rhythm in all paces. All the different movements of the test, which may last for up to ten minutes, have to be learned by heart. It is very hard for the horse because he is so fit and ready to gallop a long way next day. He has to concentrate very hard on the slow and exact paces in the small dressage arena.

Lucinda Prior-Palmer and Be Fair of Britain in the dressage test at Lühmuhlen in Germany. She won the European Championship in 1975 and in 1977.

Behind the Scenes

Walking the course is essential. Riders look at the fences and test the ground for firmness, even if it is under water.

2 Cross-Country

This is the most exciting day of the competition. There are four parts with two sections of Roads and Tracks. A horse can walk and trot along the route, and gallop the Steeplechase course. The final part is the cross-country. This is the real test of courage, skill and strength. The course may be up to 6 km long with lots of difficult jumps and natural obstacles, such as walls, banks and water.

Herbert Bloecker rides Albrant in the cross-country course at Lümuhlen. They were members of Germany's silver medal-winning team at the Montreal Olympics.

The horse's legs are often protected with bandages or boots. Thick grease helps him to slide over a fence if he hits it.

The roads and tracks phase is the longest. The horses can walk part of the way and cool down before the cross-country.

On the steeplechase phase, the time limit is very short. Horses gallop round the course which has wide brush fences.

The ten-minute break before the cross-country allows horses and riders to relax and cool off. Some horses are washed all over.

Horst Karsten of West Germany riding Sioux, makes a spectacular leap during the cross-country phase of the Munich Olympics. They were members of the team which won the bronze medal.

Bruce Davidson of the U.S.A. rides Plain Sailing (right) at the Munich Olympics. He became the World Three-Day-Event Champion in 1974.

Richard Meade rides Wayfarer through a combination fence at Crookham in Britain. He was a member of the British gold medal-winning team in the Mexico Olympics.

3 Showjumping

The final test comes after a hard day of galloping and jumping. The horse must still be fit enough to twist and turn his way round a show jumping course without knocking down any of the fences.

Princess Anne is here riding Doublet in the show jumping at Badminton in Britain. They won the European Championship in 1972 and were in the winning British team.

6

All riders have to weigh in and out to ensure they are carrying the right weight. Light riders need extra lead-filled saddle cloths.

7

After the cross-country phase, a horse is checked for injuries. A sweat rug is put on him and he is walked until quite cool.

8

On the morning of the final day, vets inspect all horses. If a horse is lame or weak, he cannot compete in the jumping.

9

Although the show jumps may look easy, horses are stiff and may be careless. They are warmed up for some time before jumping.

Other Horse Sports

There are many exciting horse sports and games. Some of them probably began soon after men first learned to ride and drive horses. Hunting and polo are many centuries old. Others, such as combined driving, are quite new. Hunting and steeplechasing have only become really popular since people have had the time to learn about horses and enjoy them.

Trotting

Trotting has developed from the ancient and very dangerous sport of chariot racing. Now breeding and training horses specially for trotting is an important business in many countries. The horses race round special tracks pulling light carriages called gigs or sulkies. A competitor in a trotting race is eliminated if his horse breaks into a canter. There are two types of trotting horses. The true trotter moves diagonally with near fore and off hind legs together. The pacer moves laterally with near fore and near hind legs together.

Scurry Driving

One of the newest types of driving competition, scurry driving is enormous fun to do or watch. A twisty course is set out in the arena, with pairs of markers, like these, set an exact distance apart. The aim is to complete the course as fast as possible, passing between the markers without touching them. The driver is allowed one passenger who can lean out at sharp corners to help balance the carriage.

Combined Driving

This competition is for teams of four horses pulling light four-wheeled carriages. It is rather like three-day eventing as it has three sections to test the driver's skills and the fitness and training of the horses. The first section is for presentation and dressage. The second is the exciting cross-country phase, with lots of hazards, as our picture shows. Finally there is an obstacle test, like the scurry driving.

Hunting

This popular sport is a good way of training for horses and riders. They learn to ride through woods and across open country at different paces, and to jump hedges, walls, banks, streams and ditches.

Steeplechasing

These exciting races, like the famous Grand National, started in the 18th century when country gentlemen challenged each other to races from one church steeple to the next, jumping the hedges in between.

Polo

Polo is one of the oldest horse sports. There are records of a similar game being played in Persia more than 2,000 years ago. The rules have changed little since then. Two teams of four riders each try to score goals by hitting a small ash or bamboo ball, only 83mm across, between two posts. The pitch is 274 metres long and 146 metres wide. In Europe, a game has six periods of play, called chukkas, each lasting seven minutes. Polo ponies are about 15.1 hands and are specially bred for speed and to be able to turn and stop quickly.

Racing Stables

Racing stables are interesting and exciting places to work, especially before a big race for one of their horses. All race horse owners hope that their horses will win races and valuable prizes. They send them to racing stables where they are carefully looked after and trained. Stables are owned by the trainer who is in charge of all the horses. He decides what sort of races are most suitable for each horse. He also plans a training programme to increase the speed and strength of each horse and make them as fit as possible for racing.

Most stable work and exercise is done by men and girls, called 'lads', who work for the trainer and may be hoping to become jockeys later. There is also a head lad who makes sure the trainer's orders are carried out. A travelling head lad is in charge of the horses on race days.

The Stable Yard

Race horses live in stables, called boxes, which surround a stable yard. The stables are large and solidly-built to be as warm and draught-free as possible. Beds of straw or wood shavings lie deep on the floor and are banked up round the walls to stop the horses from injuring themselves. The tack room, feed store and muck heap are all close to the boxes. Racing stables are busiest in the morning when all the horses, except any which are ill or have been injured, are ridden out. Usually the stable lads exercise

A Day's Training

1 Morning Feed

The head lad is up first, at about 5 a.m., to check each horse and see that all is well. He then prepares the morning feeds which are given to the horses after watering. They are then left in peace and quiet to eat and digest their food.

2 Tacked Up

The lads come on duty at about 6.30 a.m., to muck-out and brush over their first horses. Horses are then tacked-up, usually in a snaffle bridle and exercise saddle. On cold mornings they may wear a short 'quarter' sheet to keep them warm.

3 On the Gallops

The first 'lot' of horses will go out for work at first light. The lads are 'legged-up' and walk round until everyone is ready. Horses then file out in a 'string', the older ones leading. The trainer may ride with them or meet them on the gallops to watch them work. The gallops are well cared-for stretches of grass, sand or wood shavings which can be used all year round. Horses do most of their work at canter to condition their muscles, heart and lungs. They progress to 'fast work' and then to short gallops.

5 Evening Stables

Before the horses are rugged-up and given their last feeds the trainer makes an inspection. He notes the horse's condition and looks for signs of injury or strain. He may suggest that the head lad changes the horse's food.

4 Strapping

the horses. Sometimes they are ridden by the jockeys who want to get to know the horses before they ride them in a race. As well as exercising the horses, there are lots of ordinary stable jobs for the lads to do. They clean the tack, fill haynets, clean the yard and prepare the feeds. Fit race horses may need four or five feeds a day. The blacksmith visits the stables regularly to look after the horses' feet. The vet comes to examine and treat any sick horses. The afternoons are usually rest times for the horses and lads.

At about 4 p.m. the evening stable routine begins. The boxes are cleaned out and the horses given hay and water. The lad then 'straps' the horse. This is a very thorough grooming that includes massage to tone up the muscles and circulation.

Trainer's Instructions

This string of horses is on the gallops. They file around the trainer who gives instructions for each horse.

Working Upsides

A young horse may work 'upsides' an older one. This gets him used to the idea of other horses around him and encourages him to race.

At the Races

Speed contests between horses have probably been held since horses were domesticated by men. The ancient Greeks held races over 2,500 years ago but these were soon replaced by chariot racing. There are now two main sorts of racing; flat racing with no obstacles, and steeplechasing where the horses jump fences at speed. Flat racing is a summer sport when the ground is hard. The courses are short. Steeplechasing takes place in the winter when the ground is soft. The courses are longer and the horses are trained for stamina and jumping.

1 Racecourse Stables

Horses arrive early at the racecourse so they can recover from their journeys by horsebox. They are strictly guarded. Only the lads and trainers are allowed to visit them. The horses are not fed or watered for up to four hours before a race.

2 Saddling Up

Each jockey is carefully weighed, holding his saddle, before a race. The trainer then takes the saddle to a special saddling box near the paddock. The horses are taken there about 20 minutes before the race. They are saddled-up and led down to the paddock.

3 In the Paddock

Stable lads lead the horses around the parade ring in the paddock. This gives the people at the races a chance to watch the horses walking round and to decide which one they think will win. The owners of the horses and the trainers wait in the middle of the paddock for the jockeys to arrive. In this picture the signal has just been given for the jockeys to mount. The horses' rugs are taken off and their girths tightened. When all the jockeys have mounted, they go out on to the race track.

4 The Start

This is the start of a flat race. Helpers have led the horses into the stalls from the back. Sometimes horses will not go in willingly. The helpers have to push them from behind or even blindfold them. The starter then climbs on to his platform and raises his flag. Now the horses are 'under starter's orders'. Then he lowers his flag and presses a button to open the front gates of the stalls. "They're off."

5 The Finish

When several horses finish almost at the same time, it is called a close finish. Sometimes the finish is so close that the judge cannot decide which horse has won. Most racecourses have special photo-finish cameras which take pictures of the horses from both sides of the course as they gallop across the finishing line. Then the judge looks at the photographs and announces which horse has won.

6 Winners' Enclosure

Immediately after the race, the horses which have come first, second and third go back to the winners' enclosure. The jockeys dismount and take their saddles to the weighing room. The lads put sweat rugs over the horses and allow them to walk round and cool down. If there is a cup for winning the race, it will be presented to the owner.

7 Weighed In

Here is the winning jockey being 'weighed-in' by the Clerk of the Scales. This is to check that the jockeys and their saddles still weigh the same as before the race.

Lipizzaners

The pure white Lipizzaner horses of the Spanish Riding School at Vienna are one of the most beautiful and famous breeds in the world. They were first trained to be expert at high-school movements over 400 years ago, and have always been valuable and sought-after riding horses. Their great strength and light, graceful action made them the most popular horses in Europe for many centuries. Lipizzaners were originally bred in Spain by crossing Arab and Barb stallions with the native horses. Breeding continued only in the royal studs of Germany and Denmark, and at the Italian Imperial Stud at Lipizza where the most progress was made. The Spanish School was built in Vienna in 1735 and the Lipizzaners have performed there ever since, except during the First World War. Then the breeding stock was almost destroyed but a small herd was saved and returned to their home at Piber.

This is the Grand Hall of the Spanish Riding School in Vienna. It was once a royal ballroom. Beautifully decorated, it is lit by huge crystal chandeliers. These eight Lipizzaner stallions are performing a traditional quadrille. It ends with a movement called Crosswise Shifts. Each horse crosses the path of another very closely but without changing the rhythm of their paces.

Mares and Foals at Piber

All the horses for the Spanish School are bred at the Austrian National Stud Farm at Piber, high in the mountains. The foals are always dark brown or dark grey when they are born. They become whiter as they grow older, although a few foals stay dark. They leave their mothers at six months. The colts and fillies are separated when one year old. Their real schooling begins when they are over three.

Lipizzaner Brands

LINE	SIRE	DAM
PLUTO	P	
CONVERSANO	C	
NEAPOLITANO	N	
FAVORY	F	
MAETOSO	M	
SIGLAVY	S	

Lipizzaners have several brand marks to identify them. At first the horses bred at Lipizza in Italy had an 'L' brand on their left cheek. Now only horses from Piber have this mark. They also have a 'P' with a crown on their left hindquarters. These letters and signs show the horse's line or family. There are six stallion lines.

Education

Young stallions are broken with great care because they are not fully grown until they are seven years old. But they often go on working until they are over 25. Training begins at four. The horses are worked on the lungeing rein and in long-reins, like this. It helps to develop their balance and carriage —the way they move and hold themselves. Then the trainer starts riding but never for more than 45 minutes a day. He teaches the horse the rider's aids, or signals, and how to increase its forward speed. Training then becomes harder with turns, sideways movements and changes of pace.

Airs Above the Ground

Only some horses at the School become good enough to be taught 'airs above the ground'. These are spectacular rises and leaps. They were first used in battle so a horse could protect his rider by raising his front legs or leaping away from an enemy, kicking back at the same time.

The horses must first be able to perform high-school work on the ground, such as Pirouette, Piaffe and Passage. It is then decided if they are able to learn to work 'above the ground'. Their hind legs have to take all the weight off their front legs for several seconds. And a horse must be so strong and active that if he is prevented from moving forward, he rises into a Pesade, like the bay horse.

The horse in the lower picture is performing a Levade. This is a crouching rise. Other 'airs above the ground' are the Croupade, where the horse leaps forward from a Levade, and the Courbette. This is a series of forward leaps with all four legs off the ground. There are two types of jump. In the Ballotade the horse's body is level and his hind legs are slightly stretched out. The hind legs are fully stretched back for the Capriole. All the movements are done with great precision and power.

The Rodeo

At Rodeos cowboys show how good they are at riding and rounding up cattle. They can also win big prizes for other dangerous sports such as steer wrestling and bull riding.

Rodeos started about 100 years ago in the American West. After rounding up the cattle, the cowboys from several ranches would meet to have some fun. They took it in turns to show how they could rope a steer or stay on an untamed horse. The cattle were rounded up each year. Some were sold and the calves were branded with their owner's mark.

Bareback Bronco Riding

In this competition a cowboy tries to balance on the back of a bucking horse for at least eight seconds. He has no saddle and only a loop of leather to hold on to. If he can jab the horse above its shoulders with his blunt spurs, he is awarded extra points by the judges.

THE RIDER WAVES HIS FREE HAND IN THE AIR TO TRY AND KEEP HIS BALANCE. HE WILL LOSE MARKS IF HE TOUCHES ANY PART OF HIS HORSE.

HORSES ARE KEPT IN SMALL WOODEN PENS BESIDE THE ARENA, CALLED BUCKING PENS. COWBOYS DO NOT KNOW WHICH HORSE THEY WILL RIDE UNTIL JUST BEFORE THEIR TURN COMES.

1 Roping a Calf

Cowboys on round-ups have to rope calves and drag them to the branding fire. This event is a race against time to rope a calf and tie up three of its legs. First the calf is let out of its pen and then the cowboy rides out of his. The cowboy throws his rope to lasso the calf.

2

Roping horses are trained to stop immediately they see that the calf has been lassoed. The end of the rope is tied to the saddle horn. The cowboy leaps from his horse and runs to the calf while the horse pulls back all the time to keep the rope taut.

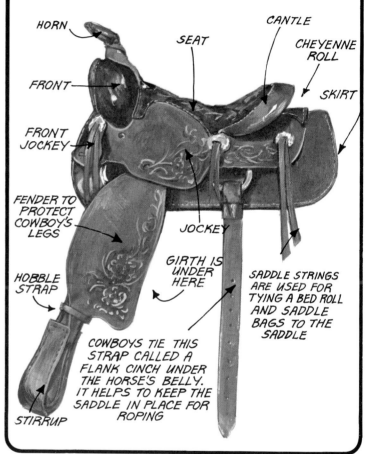

A STRAP IS TIED TIGHTLY ROUND THE HORSE JUST IN FRONT OF ITS HIND LEGS. THE HORSE KICKS AND BUCKS TO TRY AND GET RID OF THE STRAP.

A JUDGE IN THE ARENA USES SPECIAL SIGNALS TO GIVE MARKS TO BOTH THE HORSE AND THE RIDER.

A Western Saddle

Cowboys sometimes spend all day on horseback so their saddles must be very comfortable. They also have to be strong enough to hold a fighting steer tied to the saddle horn after the cowboy has lassoed it.

HORN

CANTLE

SEAT

CHEYENNE ROLL

FRONT

SKIRT

FRONT JOCKEY

FENDER TO PROTECT COWBOY'S LEGS

JOCKEY

HOBBLE STRAP

GIRTH IS UNDER HERE

SADDLE STRINGS ARE USED FOR TYING A BED ROLL AND SADDLE BAGS TO THE SADDLE

COWBOYS TIE THIS STRAP CALLED A FLANK CINCH UNDER THE HORSE'S BELLY. IT HELPS TO KEEP THE SADDLE IN PLACE FOR ROPING

STIRRUP

3

Sometimes the calf is thrown to the ground as the horse stops and the rope pulls tight round its neck. Sometimes the cowboy picks up the calf and drops it on its side. He carries a piece of rope in his mouth, called pigging string, to tie up the calf's feet.

4

As soon as the calf is lying on the ground with its legs tied, the cowboy raises his arms, and the judges record the time. The winners of these competitions can sometimes lasso a calf, dismount, throw the calf to the ground and tie it up in less than 12 seconds.

Wild Horses

All the horses which lived in the world were completely wild until about 7,000 years ago. They lived in herds, ruled over by a stallion, and were quite free and untamed. Nobody fed them, sheltered them or cared for them in any way.

Only very few completely wild horses remain today. But many thousands live in semi-wild herds in many countries. The head of the herd is the stallion, and the mares and foals are his 'family'. He finds food, water and shelter for them and teaches the foals how to survive on their own. He stands guard to warn the herd of dangers such as hunters, approaching storms or dangerous animals.

If you are lucky enough to see a herd of wild horses, the stallion will probably be on the look-out, patrolling his kingdom and scenting for danger, while the mares and foals are resting or feeding.

Lions, tigers and other members of the cat family are some of wild horses' most dangerous enemies.

Most foals are born in the spring and early summer. They can then grow strong before the winter. Sometimes a few foals are born later, but these rarely survive their first winter.

Foals wean themselves naturally. This means that they stop drinking their mother's milk and begin to eat grass. They normally stay with their mothers until their second spring. Then they are driven away when a new foal is born.

The stallion of a herd will not allow any other fully-grown male horse in his herd. He will drive them off when they are three years old. Some will wander by themselves. The weak ones die, and some form all-male rogue herds. Sooner or later a particularly strong young horse will challenge the herd leader. Sometimes he will shadow the herd for months waiting for a chance to fight.

Stallions fight with teeth and hooves and can cause terrible injuries to each other. Sometimes the herd stallion will win and drive away the younger horse. But the day will come when he will be too old and weak. Then he will be deposed. This sounds cruel. But if it did not happen, the herd would not have a leader strong enough to protect it.

The most famous truly wild horses left in the world is the herd in the Gobi desert of Western Mongolia. They were found by a 19th century explorer called Przvalski. These Przvalski horses seem to be pure descendants of the original Northern horse.

Another herd of wild horses was recently found in an

unexplored valley in South America. A rock fall is thought to have trapped the horses which have probably been there since shortly after the Spanish invasion in the 16th century.

All the herds of semi-wild horses and ponies belong to someone. Although they live completely wild most of the time, they are usually rounded up once a year for branding and drafting. Branding means that a special mark is burnt on their hides to show who they belong to. Drafting means that certain animals are taken out of the herd to be sold or trained for riding or work.

In France, there are the famous white horses of the Carmargue, the salt marshes at the mouth of the Rhône. In Britain and Ireland many native ponies live semi-wild; Shetland ponies in the Outer Hebrides, Connemaras in Galway. There are also Welsh, Dartmoor, Exmoor and New Forest ponies. In some parts of South Russia, Poland and Hungary, there is a semi-wild breed, called Tarpan. It probably dates back to the last Ice Age.

Horses live wild in the Australian outback, on the prairies of Central and Western America, and on the pampas of South America.

In 1925 a man called Aimé Tschiffley set out on a 16,000 km ride from Buenos Aires to Washington. For this great journey, he needed really tough, hardy horses. He chose two wild Criollo horses, called Mancha and Gato. Mancha was 16 and Gato was 15 years old. Mancha lived to be 40 and Gato to be 36.

A wild outdoor life is much healthier than a domesticated life, for horses and ponies which are strong enough to survive. Mountain pastures, moorlands and prairies provide lots of natural food. Spring water is much purer than piped water, and wild horses never get too fat, as they are always on the move. Their legs grow strong from steady exercise. They are not damaged by being made to gallop and jump, by being made to carry too heavy loads, and by being made to ride on roads. Their feet stay strong and trimmed by the natural rough surfaces of the ground.

Only horses born in the wild can survive in the wild. Horses, such as Thoroughbreds, which have been specially bred in captivity for many years could not survive without the food and shelter which men provide, nor without the help of people such as vets and blacksmiths. Special breeding in captivity has produced horses with extra speed, grace and softness. But strength, hardiness and courage come from wild horses.

Getting to Know a Pony

Learning to ride is great fun but there is much more to it than just sitting in a saddle. If you find out about horses and ponies and how to handle them, you will learn to ride well and happily.

Ponies are gentle but strong and should be handled quietly and firmly. They are startled by sudden noises and movements, so talk to a pony before you go up to him or touch him. Then he will get to know your voice and trust you.

1 Catching a Pony

Go into the field, taking his headcollar and a titbit, such as a sliced carrot. Remember to close the gate behind you. If a pony lives on his own, give him a call.

2

If he is with others, keep the titbit in your pocket and walk to him, talking quietly. Offer the carrot from your left hand as you slip the lead rope over his head.

Measuring a Pony

Height is measured in hands from the ground to the top of your pony's withers. One hand equals 4 ins or about 10 cms. Take off one centimetre for his shoes.

Face Markings

Star

Snip

Blaze

Stripe

Leg Markings

Sock

Stocking

Points of a Horse

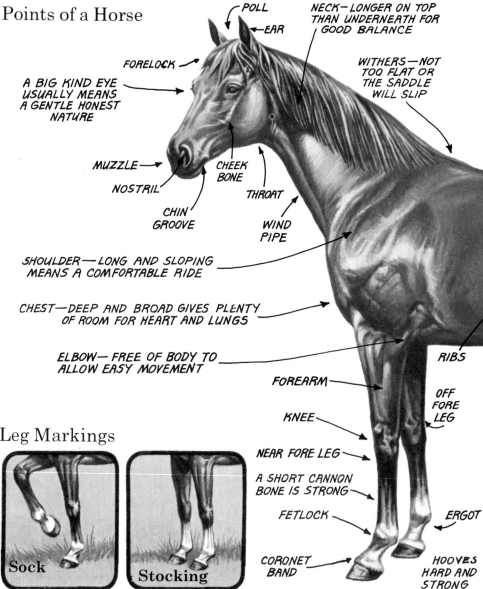

POLL

EAR

NECK—LONGER ON TOP THAN UNDERNEATH FOR GOOD BALANCE

FORELOCK

WITHERS—NOT TOO FLAT OR THE SADDLE WILL SLIP

A BIG KIND EYE USUALLY MEANS A GENTLE HONEST NATURE

MUZZLE

CHEEK BONE

NOSTRIL

THROAT

CHIN GROOVE

WIND PIPE

SHOULDER—LONG AND SLOPING MEANS A COMFORTABLE RIDE

CHEST—DEEP AND BROAD GIVES PLENTY OF ROOM FOR HEART AND LUNGS

ELBOW—FREE OF BODY TO ALLOW EASY MOVEMENT

RIBS

FOREARM

OFF FORE LEG

KNEE

NEAR FORE LEG

A SHORT CANNON BONE IS STRONG

FETLOCK

ERGOT

CORONET BAND

HOOVES HARD AND STRONG

3 While he is munching, put on the headcollar. Give him a pat and another titbit to reward him for being caught or he may not want to come to you next time.

4 Take the rope like this. Say "Walk on" and move forward. You should be able to walk at a pony's shoulder. Practise leading him from both sides.

5 Never do this. Most ponies dislike being stared in the face and pull back. You can teach a pony to walk forward by tapping his side gently with a stick as you move.

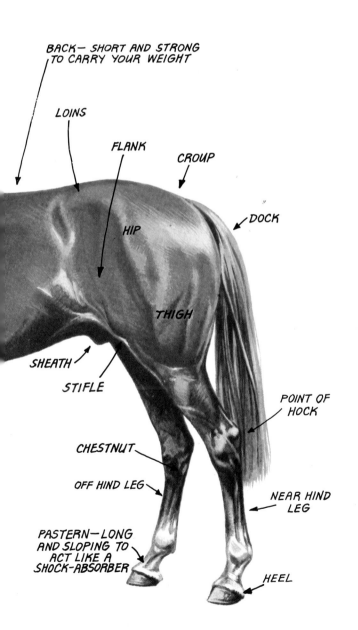

BACK— SHORT AND STRONG TO CARRY YOUR WEIGHT

LOINS

FLANK

CROUP

DOCK

HIP

THIGH

SHEATH

STIFLE

POINT OF HOCK

CHESTNUT

OFF HIND LEG

NEAR HIND LEG

PASTERN—LONG AND SLOPING TO ACT LIKE A SHOCK-ABSORBER

HEEL

Horse and Pony Colours

Black

Grey

Bay

Dun

Cream

Roan

Chestnut

Piebald

Skewbald

Saddles and Bridles

Saddles and bridles and other pieces of pony equipment are called tack. Tacks cost a lot but if you look after it well it will last for many years. Always try on new or secondhand tack if you are buying, as a pony will never be happy if it does not fit.

A saddle should fit without touching a pony's spine when your weight is on it. But check that it is not so high that the saddle is perched on his back. If it is, it will roll about and unbalance you both. It should not be too tight over his withers, nor too long over his loins. A general-purpose saddle you can use for riding and jumping, and a snaffle bridle, are probably the best to choose.

Keep the saddle on a bracket or saddle horse, and the bridle hanging by the headpiece. Store them in a dry place when you are not using them. Never leave a pony untied wearing his saddle as he may roll on it and damage it.

Parts of the Saddle

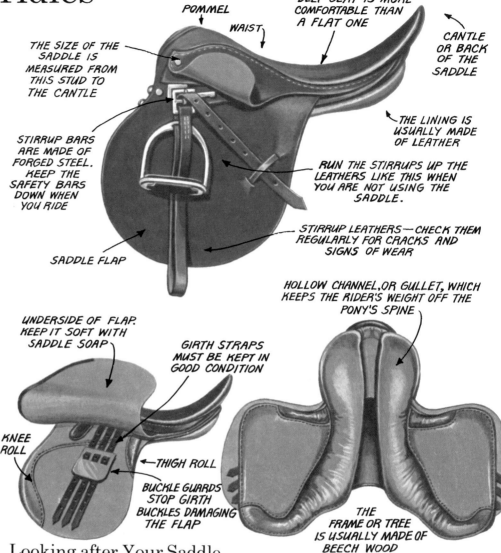

POMMEL

WAIST

SEAT—A SADDLE WITH A DEEP SEAT IS MORE COMFORTABLE THAN A FLAT ONE

CANTLE OR BACK OF THE SADDLE

THE SIZE OF THE SADDLE IS MEASURED FROM THIS STUD TO THE CANTLE

STIRRUP BARS ARE MADE OF FORGED STEEL. KEEP THE SAFETY BARS DOWN WHEN YOU RIDE

SADDLE FLAP

THE LINING IS USUALLY MADE OF LEATHER

RUN THE STIRRUPS UP THE LEATHERS LIKE THIS WHEN YOU ARE NOT USING THE SADDLE.

STIRRUP LEATHERS—CHECK THEM REGULARLY FOR CRACKS AND SIGNS OF WEAR

UNDERSIDE OF FLAP. KEEP IT SOFT WITH SADDLE SOAP

GIRTH STRAPS MUST BE KEPT IN GOOD CONDITION

KNEE ROLL

THIGH ROLL

BUCKLE GUARDS STOP GIRTH BUCKLES DAMAGING THE FLAP

HOLLOW CHANNEL, OR GULLET, WHICH KEEPS THE RIDER'S WEIGHT OFF THE PONY'S SPINE

THE FRAME OR TREE IS USUALLY MADE OF BEECH WOOD

Looking after Your Saddle

Clean your saddle after every ride. Take off the girth and stirrups. Damp-sponge off the dirt. Dry the leather, then rub in saddle soap. Polish the stirrups and clean the girth. Lastly, put everything back in place. If the saddle is new, it is a good idea to oil it to make it more supple. Every year have it checked by a saddler.

Saddling Up

1

Tie up your pony. Smooth the hair on his back, then put on the saddle, like this, from the nearside. Keep the front of the saddle well forward over his withers.

2

Slide it back into place. Go to the offside and let down the girth, checking that the flap and buckles are not caught or twisted. Return to the nearside and do up the girth.

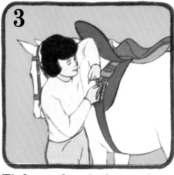

3

Tighten the girth gently, gradually smoothing the hair and skin under it. Some ponies puff themselves out, so check the girth again before and after you get on.

Removing a Saddle

Run the stirrups up the leathers. Undo the girth on the nearside, then lift off the saddle on to your left arm. Pick up the girth as it comes off and lay it across the saddle.

Girths

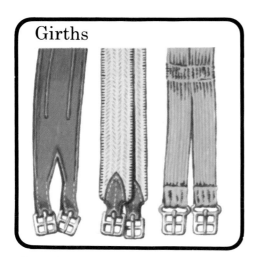

A girth is a belt which is buckled round your pony to keep the saddle in place. Good ones are made of nylon, string or leather which must be kept soft.

A Jumping Saddle

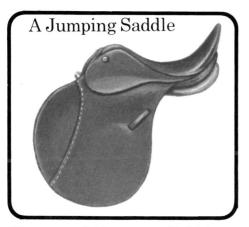

These usually have very light trees so they weigh as little as possible. They also have flaps shaped like this to help keep you in the right position for jumping.

Parts of a Bridle

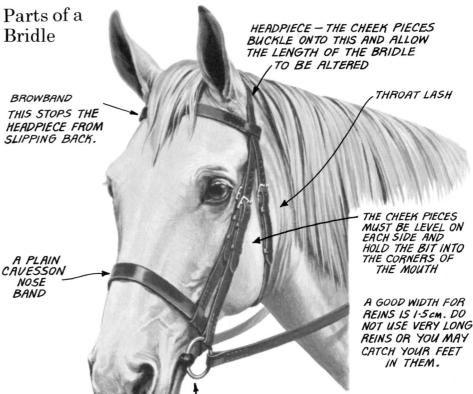

BROWBAND THIS STOPS THE HEADPIECE FROM SLIPPING BACK.

HEADPIECE – THE CHEEK PIECES BUCKLE ONTO THIS AND ALLOW THE LENGTH OF THE BRIDLE TO BE ALTERED

THROAT LASH

A PLAIN CAVESSON NOSE BAND

THE CHEEK PIECES MUST BE LEVEL ON EACH SIDE AND HOLD THE BIT INTO THE CORNERS OF THE MOUTH

A GOOD WIDTH FOR REINS IS 1·5 cm. DO NOT USE VERY LONG REINS OR YOU MAY CATCH YOUR FEET IN THEM.

A RUBBER SNAFFLE BIT IS VERY MILD. IT IS USED TO GUIDE AND STOP YOUR PONY. THINNER MOUTHPIECES ARE MORE SEVERE

Looking after Your Bridle

Wash the bit after your ride so food and saliva do not dry on it. To clean the bridle, undo all the buckles and wipe each piece separately. Dry it with a chamois leather, then rub in saddle soap with an almost dry sponge. Put it together again ready to use.

Types of Bits

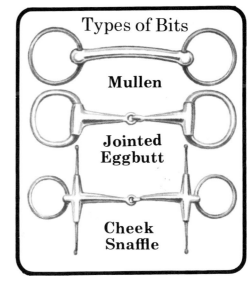

Mullen

Jointed Eggbutt

Cheek Snaffle

Fitting a Bridle

1

Slip the reins over his head, then, holding the bridle like this, open his mouth with your thumb. Gently push in the bit. At the same time, lift the headpiece over his ears.

2

Straighten his mane and lift his forelock over the browband. Check that the bit hangs level across the top of his tongue and up against his lips without wrinkling them.

3

Do up the noseband and throatlash. Your hand should fit under the throatlash, like this. Put all the straps neatly in their keepers so they will not flap about.

Removing a Bridle

Undo the noseband and throatlash. Lift the reins and headpiece gently over his ears, like this. Allow him to drop the bit from his mouth as you pull off the bridle.

A Pony of Your Own

Everyone who likes riding dreams of having their own pony. Choosing one is great fun, but takes a lot of time and has to be done carefully.

Before you buy a pony, get as much experience as you can. This will help you to know what you are looking for and choose the right one.

You also need to learn how to feed a pony, catch him in a field, groom him, and put on his saddle and bridle before you look after your own.

1 What a Pony Needs

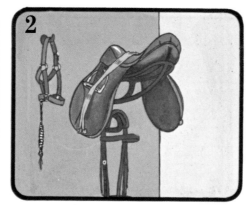

It is cheaper for you, and better for your pony, if he lives out in a field. There should be at least one acre of good grazing for each pony in the field.

2

The pony will need a saddle, bridle and a headcollar. Unless you take over the tack belonging to the pony you buy, ask your saddler to come and fit the new tack correctly.

3

4

In winter some ponies kept out at grass need a New Zealand rug. They also need extra food then. Find out if your local feed merchant can sell you hay and pony nuts.

5

Every four to six weeks, the blacksmith should take off your pony's shoes, trim his feet and replace the worn shoes with new ones. This takes about an hour.

6

Your pony should be treated for worms every eight to ten weeks to keep him healthy. Once a year the vet should inject him against 'flu and tetanus and check his health.

7

Here are some of the things you will need for grooming your pony. It is a good idea to get them before you buy a pony. If you look after them, they will last a very long time.

Choosing the Right Size

It is better to buy a pony that is a little too big for you at first. Then you can still ride him as you grow older. But he should not be so big you cannot control him. If your pony is too small, you will not be comfortable and he may not be able to carry you for long. If you want to ride in competitions, make sure your pony's height is not over the class limit.

Pony Too Big

Pony Too Small

What to Look For

The more you know about a pony before you buy it, the better. Look for one whose owner has outgrown it or one you already know, perhaps from a local riding school. Take someone with you who knows a lot about horses.

Do not buy at an auction as you cannot ride the ponies. Choose a pony that is between 6 and 14 years old and has been fully schooled. See him in a field. Is he friendly and easy to catch? Have him saddled and ridden. Then ride him.

If he seems to like being ridden and walks quietly in noisy traffic, ask a good horse vet to check that he is healthy. If all is well and you are sure this is the pony you want, then you can go ahead and buy him.

Enjoying a Pony

You will enjoy riding on an ordinary steady pony. You can also compete in many events at local gymkhanas and Pony Club rallies. Ponies usually enjoy hunting and jumping natural fences, such as

logs and ditches. Most can learn quite easily to jump a course of show jumps up to about one metre high. But highly-trained show jumpers are very expensive. They need courage to tackle big jumps

and so may be too excitable to be good first ponies. Showing classes are like beauty contests—ponies must look good and move well.

Keeping a Pony at Grass

Ponies are happier living with others, so try to share your field with a friend who has one too. Make sure they have food, water and shelter.

Your field should be fenced with post and rails, strong hedges or plain wire. Be careful with barbed wire as it can easily injure a pony. Wire should be pulled very tight with the bottom strand at least 46 cm high.

Ponies like to eat short juicy grass. They do not like the long coarse grass where droppings have fallen.

If you do not look after your field, it may become "horse sick". This means that the parts which ponies eat are bare, and other parts are covered in long, useless grass. Ponies get worms if they eat the eggs of worms which live in droppings. It is a good idea to clear up droppings regularly. It helps to let cows graze the field and eat the long grass.

A shelter like this, facing South, is ideal. But a thick hedge on the north side of a field is good enough shelter for most ponies.

The best water supply is a trough which fills up automatically as your pony drinks. It should be cleaned out regularly.

Check your pony often for injuries. Pick out his feet. See that his shoes are in good order.

The gate must be strong and have a catch that ponies cannot undo. It is wise to have a chain and padlock as well.

1 Extra Feeding

Your pony will need hay when grass is scarce and has little goodness in it. This is usually from October to May. Putting it in a hay net hitched up high, like this, saves waste. He will need between 2½ and 5 kilos a day, depending on his size. Always feed hay which has a sweet smell. Mouldy hay could make your pony ill or damage his breathing.

2

Ponies that look well when fed on hay alone, may not need anything else. But if your pony is working hard he will need extra food, such as nuts. They are easy to use but expensive. Feed from about 1 kilo to a very small pony up to 3 kilos to a 14 hand pony, split into 2 small feeds. Read about other sorts of food on the next two pages.

Some ponies enjoy a salt or mineral lick. Put a block in a sheltered place for him.

This is a post-and-rail fence. It is the best for ponies as it is strong and they cannot injure themselves on it.

Never tie a pony to a fence, in case he is frightened and pulls it down.

Poisonous Plants

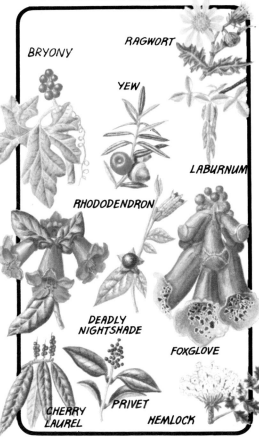

BRYONY

RAGWORT

YEW

LABURNUM

RHODODENDRON

DEADLY NIGHTSHADE

FOXGLOVE

CHERRY LAUREL

PRIVET

HEMLOCK

Search your field and hedges for poisonous plants before putting your pony in. Uproot any you find and burn them. Put a fence round any harmful shrubs or trees to keep them out of reach. Too many acorns are poisonous but most ponies do not eat them.

Grooming

Brush off dry mud with a dandy brush, but do not brush too much as this will remove the natural grease which keeps your pony dry and warm. Tidy his mane and tail, sponge his eyes, nose and dock and pick out his feet.

Cold Weather

Your pony can stay outside even in weather like this, as long as he has extra food to keep him warm. Give him at least as much as a stabled pony. When it freezes, do not forget to break the ice on his water trough every day.

A New Zealand Rug

This is a waterproof rug which your pony can wear during the winter, if he is part-clipped or if he does not grow a thick coat. Make sure it fits correctly and check it every day or it may begin to rub and make him sore.

Stables and Feeding

If you ride a lot and your pony needs to be really fit, it is best to keep him stabled. Clip his thick winter coat so he does not sweat and lose weight, and keep him warm with a rug.

There is no need to keep him in all the time. A few hours a day in the field will keep him happy and easy to manage. Try to stick to a regular routine, such as this, which suits you and your pony:
7.30 am—Give water, a feed, a small haynet and muck out.
10.00 am—Brush your pony, pick out his feet, exercise for at least an hour. 12.00—Small feed and turn out till tea time.
4.00 pm—Groom thoroughly, bed down. About 5.00 pm—Fill water bucket, and haynet, give evening feed. Before you go to bed check all is well.

The Stable

A loose box, like this, with a divided door is ideal. A strong shed can often be used. It should be at least 3 x 4 metres, with a high roof and a doorway 1.20 metres wide. Rough concrete, to stop him slipping, makes a good floor. It should slope down slightly towards the drain.

Feeding

Ponies have small stomachs for their size so they need to eat little and often. The basic food that replaces grass for stabled ponies is hay, which is a bulk food. They also need other sorts of food to give them energy. All ponies need different amounts.

Good hay should have a sweet smell, and be crisp to feel. Never feed musty or mouldy hay, nor hay that is less than six months old. Give less energy food if you cannot exercise your pony. Be sure he has water to drink before each feed.

Energy Foods

These are the most important part of a hard working pony's diet. They make him strong and fit and ready to work.

Barley

This is a good fattening food but not so heating as oats. Feed it well crushed or boil whole grains for 2–3 hours.

Oats

These can make ponies hot and excitable, so feed only small amounts, well crushed, to begin with. They should be clean, and at least six months old.

Maize

This is not so full of protein as oats but should still only be fed in very small quantities.

Looking after the Stable

Cover the floor with deep bedding to keep your pony comfortable and warm. Wheat straw is best, except for a greedy pony who may eat it and get too fat or even ill. Peat, wood shavings, sawdust or shredded paper are also good.

Muck out each morning. Remove the droppings and wet straw. Stack the clean straw in a corner and brush the floor. Re-lay the bed, banking it round the walls. Add clean straw when it is needed, which may not be every day.

Tools You Will Need

Buy good tools that you can handle easily. Use a basket or skep to carry droppings from the stable. You will also need a broom, a shovel and at least one fork. Do not use a fork with sharp prongs as this could be dangerous.

Rugging Up

A jute rug is usually put on a clipped pony at night, in winter, with one or two underblankets. In daytime, a woollen rug is useful inside, and a New Zealand rug for outside. Throw it on like this.

Make sure it is well forward. Then do up the front buckle. From the back, pull the rug into place. Walk round to the off side to make sure that the rug is hanging evenly and is not caught up.

Put on the roller and do it up tight enough to keep the rug in place. Smooth out any creases. To take off the rug, remove the roller, undo the front buckle and slide it off backwards.

Bulk Foods

These are parts of your pony's diet which help to fill him up. They also stop him eating the energy food too quickly.

Sugar Beet Pulp

This must be soaked for 24 hours before feeding.

Chaff

This is hay which has been put through a chaff cutter. This should be done little and often or chaff will become dusty.

Bran

Bran is a useful bulk food. It is the ground outer husks of wheat. It can be fed dry with oats or damp in a mash. Warm bran mash is good for sick ponies.

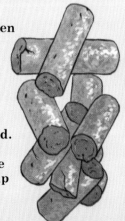

Nuts

There are lots of different sorts of pony nuts. Mostly they are a ready-made mixture of energy and bulk food which gives your pony the same balanced diet all the time. There are other sorts, called low-protein nuts which are mainly dried grass. They are all easy to store and feed. Some fresh greenery or vegetables each day will help his digestion.

Grooming

There are two kinds of grooming. They are brushing to remove mud and make the pony look tidy; and deep grooming which cleans and massages the skin and helps to keep your pony fit and healthy. If your pony lives at grass, use only a dandy brush, or you will remove the waterproof grease from his coat. Pick out his feet before you ride. If your pony is stabled, deep groom him every day after your ride. Then the pores of his skin are open and the scurf loose.

Speak quietly, then run your hand down the leg from shoulder to fetlock and pick up the foot. Use the hoof pick from heel to toe to get anything that is lodged there.

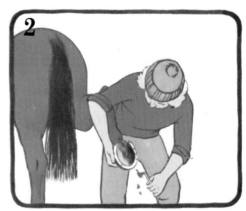

Slide your hand down the back of the lower leg and lift the hind foot in the same way. Clean out the foot like this, taking care not to hurt the sensitive frog.

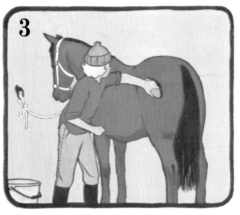

Brush off mud and sweat stains with a dandy brush. This has hard bristles and will also bring scurf to the surface. Use short, firm strokes except in tender parts.

Deep groom with a body brush, using short circular strokes with your weight behind the brush. Clean the brush with the curry comb after every few strokes.

Carefully wipe round his eyes and nostrils with a damp sponge, or cotton wool which you throw away. Clean under his tail using another sponge kept just for this job.

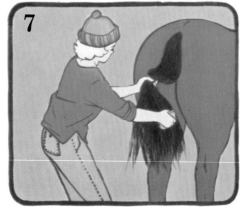

Put the mane on the wrong side, then brush it back into place, a few hairs at a time. Brush the tail like this, with a body brush. Take care not to break any hairs.

Put a coat of hoof oil on the hoof wall. Put it also on the sole and frog if you have washed and dried them. This looks good and helps to stop them cracking.

Use a damp water brush to lay the mane and untidy hairs at the top of the tail. Lastly, wipe your pony all over with a clean cloth so his coat is smooth and shiny.

Health

Most ponies are tough. If you take good care and feed them sensibly, they will probably be healthy. But illness and accidents can happen, so learn what to look for and when to call the vet. A healthy pony has a shiny coat, bright eyes and eats well. Look out for signs of lameness, poor appetite or a dull coat. Notice if he is losing weight or putting on too much. Start your own First Aid kit with cotton wool, wound powder, antiseptic ointment and bandages.

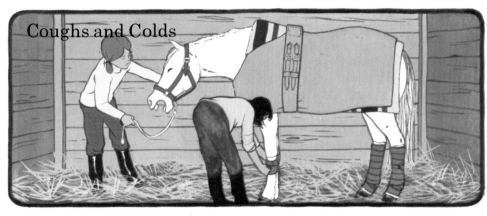

Coughs and Colds

If your pony starts coughing, keep him alone so he does not infect others. Send for the vet. Colds last about 10 days, but your pony must be rested for several weeks.

Keep him warm and offer tasty food, such as warm damp mashes with glycerine, honey or treacle to soothe his throat. Cut out hard food. Rest a pony with a cough.

Colic

This is a tummy pain and is sometimes due to bad feeding. It may be very serious. Call the vet immediately and keep your pony warm and moving until he comes.

Laminitis

Ponies which eat too rich grass sometimes suffer from this. Tender parts in the front feet swell and become so sore it hurts them to walk. Call the vet.

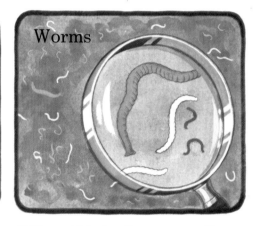

Worms

Different kinds of worms can live inside your pony, eat his food and get into his bloodstream. They will make him thin and unhealthy if he is not treated regularly.

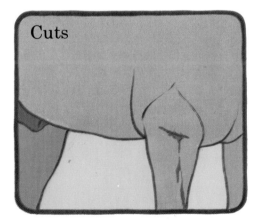

Cuts

Bathe small cuts in mild antiseptic and warm water. Dry the cut and put on wound powder. Deep cuts may need stitching by the vet and the pony kept in and rested.

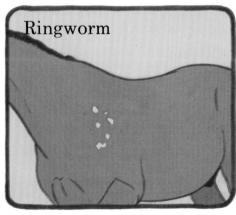

Ringworm

Small, round, bare patches appear anywhere on the body. It is very catching, so isolate him and handle in rubber gloves. Ask your vet for something to help clear it up.

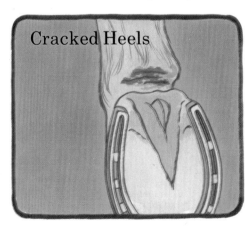

Cracked Heels

Wet pastures or too much washing can give your pony sore heels. Try to keep them clean and dry, and ask your vet for a suitable healing cream.

At the Blacksmith

Horses which run wild do not need shoes. Their hooves wear down naturally. But horses which work or travel on hard roads need their feet protected by metal shoes. The hard outside of the horse's hoof grows about 5 mm each month. This needs to be trimmed or the horse may go lame.
To do this, the blacksmith takes off the old shoe, cuts off the extra growth, and fits a new shoe.

An electric fan behind the forge blows air into the fire to make it hotter.

The blacksmith cuts long pieces of fullered iron into short lengths to make horseshoes.

Water to cool hot horseshoes.

Blacksmiths wear leather aprons to protect their clothes from wear and sparks.

This blacksmith is hammering a red hot shoe into shape.

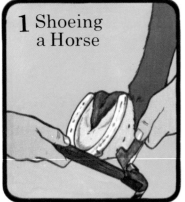

1 Shoeing a Horse

First the blacksmith uses the sharp edge of a buffer to loosen the nails which are holding the old shoe on to the horse's hoof.

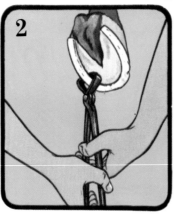

2

Then he levers off the old shoe with pincers, taking care not to twist it sideways or damage the outside wall of the hoof.

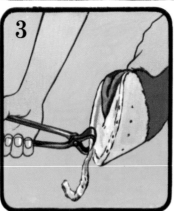

3

He uses clippers, called hoof parers, to cut away the extra wall which has grown since the last time the horse was shod.

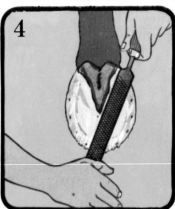

4

To make quite sure that both sides are level and that the new shoe will fit comfortably, the blacksmith rasps the hoof.

46

Being a blacksmith is a very difficult job to learn. Young men, called apprentices, train for many years before they are good enough to make and fit horseshoes on their own.

This blacksmith is holding a horse's hind leg and rasping the hoof.

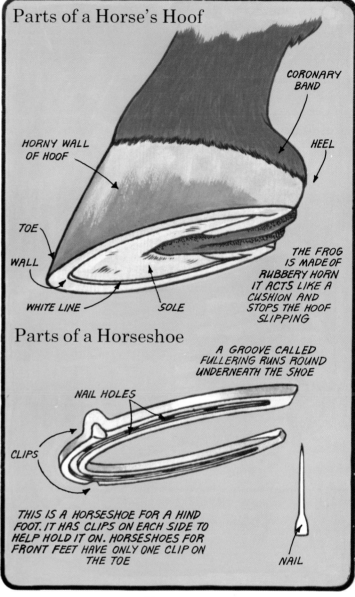

Parts of a Horse's Hoof

CORONARY BAND

HORNY WALL OF HOOF

HEEL

TOE

WALL

WHITE LINE

SOLE

THE FROG IS MADE OF RUBBERY HORN IT ACTS LIKE A CUSHION AND STOPS THE HOOF SLIPPING

Parts of a Horseshoe

A GROOVE CALLED FULLERING RUNS ROUND UNDERNEATH THE SHOE

NAIL HOLES

CLIPS

NAIL

THIS IS A HORSESHOE FOR A HIND FOOT. IT HAS CLIPS ON EACH SIDE TO HELP HOLD IT ON. HORSESHOES FOR FRONT FEET HAVE ONLY ONE CLIP ON THE TOE

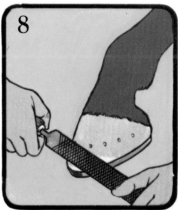

5 He presses the hot shoe on to the hoof to make sure it fits exactly. The wall of the hoof has no feeling so it does not hurt.

6 Now the blacksmith nails on the new shoe so that the points of the nails stick out about 3 cm up the wall of the hoof.

7 When the points of the nails have been twisted off, he hammers them from underneath, holding pincers under the ends.

8 Finally he rasps the outside of the hoof and the points of the nails, called clenches, so there are no sharp edges.

In the Saddle

Always remember to wear a hard hat whenever you go riding. Before you mount your pony, make sure that the girth is tight enough or your saddle may slip round. Try to sit with your knees and thighs close against the saddle, ready to grip and keep you steady. Once you learn to do this, you will not be tempted to use the reins to keep your balance.

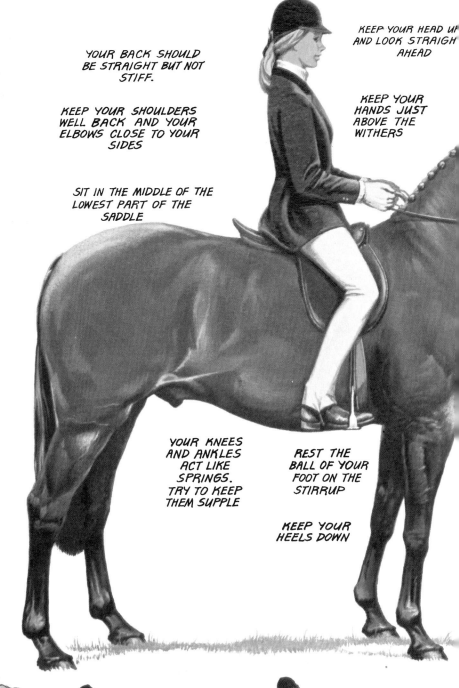

YOUR BACK SHOULD BE STRAIGHT BUT NOT STIFF.

KEEP YOUR HEAD UP AND LOOK STRAIGH AHEAD

KEEP YOUR SHOULDERS WELL BACK AND YOUR ELBOWS CLOSE TO YOUR SIDES

KEEP YOUR HANDS JUST ABOVE THE WITHERS

SIT IN THE MIDDLE OF THE LOWEST PART OF THE SADDLE

YOUR KNEES AND ANKLES ACT LIKE SPRINGS. TRY TO KEEP THEM SUPPLE

REST THE BALL OF YOUR FOOT ON THE STIRRUP

KEEP YOUR HEELS DOWN

Tightening Your Girth

Move your leg forward and lift the saddle flap. Pull up the straps one at a time, pushing the spike of the buckle into the higher hole.

Mounting

1

Stand beside your pony's near shoulder, facing his tail. Hold the reins in your left hand with a handful of mane, like this. Hold the stirrup with the other hand and put the ball of your left foot into the stirrup iron.

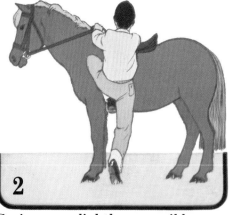

2

Spring up as lightly as possible, taking care not to jab your pony's side with your left foot. Hold either the front or back of the saddle with your right hand.

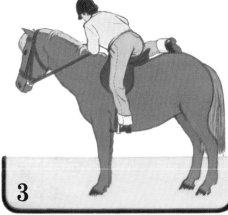

3

As you straighten your left knee, swing your right leg up off the ground and clear over your pony's rump. Take care not to touch him with your foot on the way over.

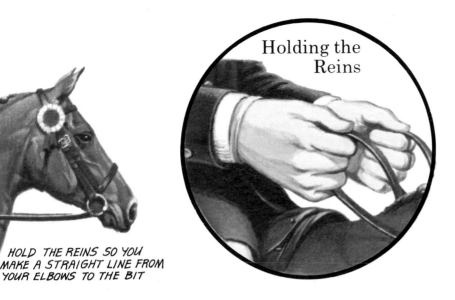

Holding the Reins

HOLD THE REINS SO YOU MAKE A STRAIGHT LINE FROM YOUR ELBOWS TO THE BIT

Holding the Reins

Your hands are the most important link between you and your pony. Hold the reins lightly so you can just feel your pony's mouth. From the bit, the reins should pass between your third and little fingers, across the palms of your hands and be held between your thumbs and first fingers.

Keep your hands level, one on each side of your pony's neck about 10 cms apart. Hold the reins with your knuckles facing the front and your thumbs on top like this.

Dismounting

Adjusting Your Stirrups

Pull up the loose end of the stirrup leather, holding one finger on the spike of the buckle. Now you can move the leather up or down without losing the end.

1 Take both feet out of the stirrups so your legs are hanging free. Now lean slightly forward and, still holding the reins, rest your left hand on the pony's mane.

2 With your right hand on the front of the saddle, lean slightly forward. Then swing your right leg backwards and clear over your pony's loins.

4 Sit down gently into the saddle so you do not hurt or frighten your pony. Put your right foot into the stirrup iron and take up the reins in both hands.

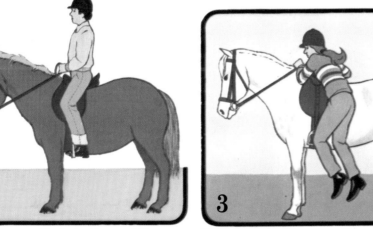

3 Slide gently down, well away from your pony's front legs. Remember it is dangerous to dismount by swinging your right leg forward over your pony's neck.

4 Run up the stirrup irons and take the reins over your pony's head. To lead, hold the end of the reins in your left hand and both reins close to the bit with your right.

49

Paces

Ponies have four paces—walk, trot, canter and gallop. Learn to ride them correctly, then you and your pony will be comfortable and will work happily together.

Walking

The walk is the easiest pace because it is calm and steady. You have time to think about the right way to ride. It may feel quite strange at first, but the secret is to relax just enough to feel the rhythm of your pony's stride. Hold on to the saddle or mane until you feel safe, then take the reins. These are to control and guide your pony, not to hold you on.

As your pony walks, his head moves up and down. Hold the reins very lightly so that your hands can follow his rhythm. Sit well down in the saddle and try not to lean forward or look down.

The walk has four hoof beats. Each hoof strikes the ground separately in turn like this—near fore, off hind, off fore, near hind.

How a Pony Walks

Trotting

Trotting is more bouncy and may feel uncomfortable until you learn to rise. Do not try trotting until you have learned to walk. You can either sit down to trot or rise up and down in the saddle, in time with the pony's movements.

Rising to the trot is easy once you get it right. Let the bounce of your pony's stride push you up and forward a little from your knees. Then sit back gently into the saddle in a regular rhythm. Try to keep your hands and lower legs quite still. All this takes a lot of practice. It may help to say "Up-down" in time with your pony's stride at first. Lean slightly forward so you do not lose your balance. Keep your back straight but not stiff.

Your pony's legs move in pairs. The near fore leg and off hind leg together, then the off fore leg and near hind leg together. These are called diagonals.

How a Pony Trots

Cantering

Cantering is exciting and is the favourite pace for most riders. Remember, though, it is quite tiring, so practise for only a short time at first.

To begin with, hold the saddle with one hand. Sit up straight and allow your hips to go with the movement of the pony, so your seat stays in the saddle. You will be stiff at first and find it hard not to bounce up and down. Your hands must hold the reins so your pony's head can swing up and down with the stride.

A pony can canter with either fore leg leading. When cantering in a circle, the inside leg should lead, then he will be properly balanced. The canter has three hoof beats. When the off fore leg leads, as in the picture, the hoof beats are near hind, then off hind and near fore together, and then off fore.

How a Pony Canters

Galloping

The gallop is the fastest and most exciting pace. You should gallop only if your pony is fit and you can control him when cantering.

Ponies increase their speed from canter to gallop by taking longer strides. They push harder with their hind legs and stretch out their body, neck and head. Each foot is on the ground for a shorter time, and there is a moment when all four feet are off the ground at once.

Take your weight forward and right out of the saddle to give your pony's back the freedom to make the extra effort. Have your weight on your knees and feet. Never gallop where there are people walking or where you might lose control of your pony.

As in the canter, your pony's inside leg should lead if you are on a bend. The gallop has four hoof beats. When the off fore leg leads, the hoof beats are—near hind, off hind, near fore, off fore.

How a Pony Gallops

Aids

Every well-trained pony has been taught to understand a special set of signals from its rider. These signals are called aids. You must learn them so you can tell your pony what to do. Signals using your voice, hands, legs and body are called natural aids. Whips and spurs are artificial aids. You need quite a lot of practice to use these aids correctly. It is important that you learn on a trained pony which understands and obeys. Then you get the feel of doing things right.

Voice

Talk quietly but firmly. Your pony will learn to understand your tone and become confident, as long as you treat him well. Always keep your commands very simple. He will understand the sound of words such as "Walk" and "Trot" and "Whoa" but not long sentences.

Hands

Your hands help to control and guide your pony. Use your fingers to send messages along the reins telling him what to do. Never use the reins to hold you on. Try not to pull at your pony with the reins. This will make his mouth hard and he will soon begin to pay no attention when you tell him what to do.

Body

You can change the balance of your pony by moving your body slightly. If you change the pressure of your seat on the saddle, he will soon learn to understand what you are telling him to do. The exercises at the bottom of the page and lots of practice on the lunge will help you to control your movements.

Legs

Use the lower part of your legs to tell your pony when to go faster. Squeeze against his sides just behind the girth, using different amounts of pressure. You control his hind-quarters by squeezing further back behind the girth. This helps to tell him when to move sideways or turn.

Exercises

It may seem difficult and tiring at first to ride the right way. This is because you are using muscles which do not often have to work. Try these exercises to help make you supple and fit. They are all great fun and will help to improve your riding. Practise for only a few minutes on a quiet pony somewhere safe, or with someone to hold your pony steady. Tie a knot in your reins so you do not catch your toe in them as you move about.

Rising in the Saddle

Lean slightly forward keeping your head up. Push down and raise your seat about 5 cms from the saddle. Then lower it gently. Hold your pony's mane at first if necessary.

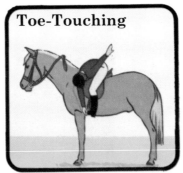

Toe-Touching

Bend down and touch your toes like this. First one side then the other. Make sure your foot does not come up to meet your hand. Do not let your other leg slip backwards.

Swinging Arms

Swing round to face one side then the other, with your arms at shoulder height. Do it in a smooth rhythm, keeping your legs quite still. Try arm circling too.

First Lessons

The girl in this picture is having a lesson on a lungeing rein. The instructor has control of the pony so she does not need to hold the reins. When you do this, you will really be able to feel your pony's movements. Hold on to the front of the saddle if you feel unsafe. A short lesson in each direction is enough, or your muscles become tired and stiff. It is important that you are lunged by someone experienced, and on a pony that goes well. Then you will be able to concentrate on keeping your balance and riding correctly.

Do not sit stiffly. Allow your body to move with the pony.

A lungeing cavesson is put on over the bridle. The rein must be at least 4.5 metres long. It has a swivel clip which is attached to a ring on the noseband.

On a left circle, the instructor holds the rein in his left hand and carries a whip in his right. His voice is usually enough to control the pony's speed.

1 Leaning Back

Lean forwards, from your waist. Then bend slowly backwards until you are resting on your pony's hindquarters. Do not let your legs slip forward.

2

Now return slowly to the correct position. Keep your arms folded all the time. This is difficult if you are not fit. It helps to make your back and stomach muscles strong.

1 Around the World

Swing your right leg over your pony's neck so you are sitting side saddle. Next swing your left leg, then your right leg, over his back so you are side saddle on the other side.

2

Lastly, swing your left leg over his neck to get you back where you started. Do this in a gentle rhythm. taking care not to kick your pony. Then try it going the other way.

Changing Pace

Changes from one pace to another should be smooth without any jerky movement. Make each signal clear and just strong enough for your pony to understand and obey. Watch a good rider on a well-trained horse. The aids are almost invisible and this is what you should aim for. It takes lots of practice and can only be learned properly on a well-trained pony who will understand what you want it to do.

Increases of Pace

IF YOUR PONY TRIES TO MOVE BEFORE YOU GIVE THE SIGNAL, CHECK HIM BY INCREASING THE PRESSURE OF YOUR FINGERS ON THE REINS

KEEP YOUR HEAD UP

TRY NOT TO BECOME STIFF

Prepare to Walk

LET YOUR HANDS FOLLOW THE MOVEMENTS OF HIS HEAD

KEEP A CONTACT WITH HIS MOUTH

Walk On

As he sets off, lighten the contact on his mouth with your hands following the natural movement of his head. Don't lose contact completely or you will have no control.

Give a quick squeeze with the lower part of your legs and say "Walk on". As he sets off, slacken the reins so his head can move in the rhythm of his walk. Keep sitting up straight as he moves off.

Decreases of Pace

TRY TO SIT STILL THEN YOU WILL NOT UNBALANCE YOUR PONY

WHEN YOU FEEL HIM RESPOND TO YOUR SIGNAL, RELAX YOUR FINGERS

Canter to Trot

USE YOUR LEGS TO KEEP HIM MOVING STRAIGHT AND STOP HIS HIND QUARTERS SWINGING OUT

TAKE CARE NOT TO BOUNCE FORWARD AND LOSE CONTROL

Trot to Walk

Straighten your back and press down with your seat. At the same time, increase your feel on the reins and say slowly. "Trot". Keep your legs close to his sides so he comes to a smooth well-balanced trot.

As before, sit to the trot and press your seat down. Gently resist with your hands as you say "Walk". Bring your legs against his sides to keep him going forward as he comes into a walk.

FOR A SMOOTH CHANGE OF PACE FROM WALK TO TROT, SIT THE FIRST FEW STRIDES. START TO RISE ONCE YOUR PONY IS TROTTING IN A STEADY RHYTHM

KEEP YOUR HEELS LOW AND RISE FROM YOUR KNEES

SIT DEEP IN THE SADDLE AND PUSH WITH YOUR SEAT

"ASK" WITH THE RIGHT REIN AND GIVE FIRM PRESSURE WITH YOUR LEFT LEG BEHIND THE GIRTH

USE YOUR INSIDE LEG ON THE GIRTH TO KEEP HIM GOING FORWARD

DO EXACTLY THE OPPOSITE TO CANTER TO THE LEFT

Trot

Canter

Your pony will shorten his neck slightly as he trots, so shorten the reins before squeezing with your legs. Drive him forward with your seat and legs. Repeat the leg pressure to keep up a steady pace.

Sit deep into the saddle. Use your inside leg on the girth to keep him going forward. Take the outside leg back behind the girth. Squeeze with the inside rein to make him strike off on the required rein.

DO NOT LET YOUR FEET SLIP FORWARD. PUSH DOWN INTO YOUR HEELS

REMEMBER YOU ARE GIVING HIM A SIGNAL TO STOP— NOT PULLING HIM TO A STANDSTILL

SAY "BACK" AND KEEP HIM STRAIGHT WITH YOUR LEGS

TWO OR THREE STEPS ARE ENOUGH. THEN MAKE HIM WALK FORWARD

Halt

Rein Back

Straighten your back and increase your feel on the reins, saying "Whoa". Press with your legs to bring his hind legs under his body. This will bring him to halt standing square on all four legs.

This can only be done with a well-trained pony. Keep him standing straight with his attention on you. Give light leg aids, but resist with your hands so he steps backwards instead of forwards.

Changing Direction

It is important to be able to ride your pony smoothly to right and left at each pace. You may find it harder to turn or circle one way than the other because he is stiff on one side. Exercises can help to make him supple.

Do not lean forward and pull him round. Sit well down in the saddle. Your seat and legs tell him what to do and your hands guide him. These pictures show how to turn right. Do exactly the opposite to turn left.

Turning to the Right

Sit up straight. Keep your seat square on the saddle or you will upset your pony's balance.

Your pony should look to the right by bending his neck, not just by turning his head to the side.

Hind feet should follow in the tracks of front feet.

How Ponies Bend their Spines

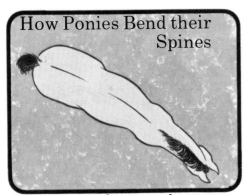

To turn or circle correctly, a pony should bend his neck and spine in the direction in which he is going. Seen from above, his body makes an arc, like this.

What Your Hands Do

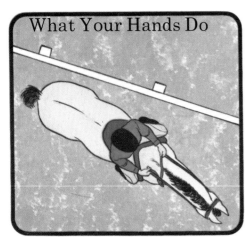

Guide your pony by increasing pressure on the right rein. Give a little with your left hand to allow for the turn. But still keep enough contact to control him.

What Your Right Leg Does

The inside leg stays in the normal place close to the girth. Your pony should seem to bend himself round this leg as he turns. Keep up a steady pace.

What Your Left Leg Does

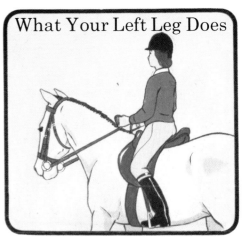

This is the outside leg. Press it lightly against your pony's side further back than usual. This stops the hindquarters swinging out to the left.

Changing the Rein

This simply means turning and riding in another direction. Try to do it as smoothly as possible, without changing your pony's rhythm. To change from the left to right rein, follow the blue line on the menage plan below. Turn diagonally across the school at the first side marker after you have ridden along the short side of the school. When you reach the marker diagonally across the school, it is easy to change to the right rein. You can also go straight across. In a group, the leading rider makes the change.

What is a Manege?

This is any enclosed area where you can practise riding without being disturbed.

An indoor riding school is ideal, but any flat level area will do. You can use a quiet corner of a field marked off with bales of straw or oil cans. The usual size is 20 × 40 metres. Certain points round the manege are marked with letters. As these are always the same, it is a good idea to learn them by heart. Then you will know what to do without looking when given an instruction.

Exercises

Ride these exercises very thoroughly for regular short training periods. They will help to make your pony supple and improve your balance. Do them first at a walk, then a steady trot. Keep up the same speed and rhythm. It is not easy to ride circles exactly. Large ones are easier, so start with these. Imagine that a circle has been drawn on the ground. Look ahead and try to keep your pony on it. Next try a figure-of-eight, which is two circles with a change of direction in the middle. Lastly try a serpentine all the way up the school.

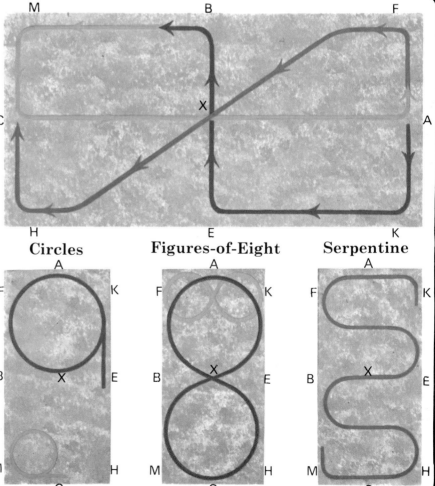

Circles   **Figures-of-Eight**   **Serpentine**

Learning to Jump

Jumping is great fun. But do not start until you feel secure and can control your pony at walk, trot and canter. It is a good idea to follow a plan of training, like the one below, with a teacher if possible.

Practice for short periods or your pony may get bored. Always finish when he has done something well. Have your stirrups a hole or two shorter to ride in the jumping position.

Approach

It is important to get the approach right, otherwise your pony will find it difficult to jump. Ride in the correct jumping position. Let your pony lower his head to judge the position and height of the jump

Take-Off

Make sure that you are not left behind as your pony pushes up and forward. Lean forward, but keep close to the saddle, and do not stand up in the stirrups. Move your hands forward to give him plenty of rein.

Trotting Poles

This is a good way to start. It will help to improve your balance and make you more confident. Your pony will learn to adjust his stride, which is important for jumping. Use solid poles 10-15 cms in diameter and at least 3 metres long. Then your pony will really have to pick up his feet to trot over them. The second pony is following quite closely to encourage him. Once ponies know what to do, they should go one at a time.

Starting Off

Start by walking over one pole. Add more, one at a time, about 1.2 metres apart. Lean forward a little and keep a light feel on your pony's mouth.

A Line of Poles

Now try at a steady rising trot. Start with one pole and then add others as before. Trot over the middle of the poles, keeping up the same rhythm all the way.

Your First Jump

When you and your pony feel safe over trotting poles, place a low cavaletto about 2.4 metres from the last pole. Trot down the line and straight over the jump.

In the Air

Sit still with your knees close to the saddle. Try not to let your lower legs slip backwards—then he will not be unbalanced. He begins to reach downwards with his front legs after he has folded his hind legs to clear the jump.

Landing

His head and neck come up to balance him as he lands. His front feet hit the ground hard. You can take some of the strain off his front legs by gently moving your shoulders and seat back just a little as you land.

Away

His front feet move off into the first stride as his hind feet come down almost in their place. Take control as soon as you land. The whole jump should be a smooth, flowing rhythm. You will find this much easier on an experienced pony.

Cavaletti

The Italian cavalry first thought of these. They wanted fences they could move easily and use to build many different jumps. Now almost all riders use them to train their horses. Work over Cavaletti will develop your pony's muscles and train him to think calmly about jumping. You can practice your jumping position and get the feel of your pony's stride. Do not follow the pony in front too closely.

How Cavaletti are Made

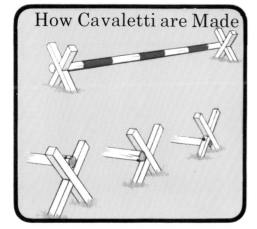

You can buy Cavaletti or make your own. Make the cross-pieces with 75 cm lengths of wood 7 x 7 cm. Then fix a pole or piece of timber 3 metres long in between.

Other Cavaletti Jumps

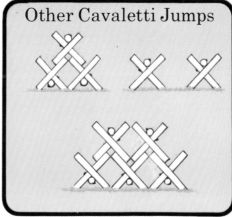

You can make lots of different jumps with your Cavaletti. Make them low and easy to jump. Then your pony will enjoy it and not start the bad habit of refusing.

Cavaletti for Cantering

This needs quite a lot of skill. Use a pole and one Cavaletto first. Then add another about 2.8 metres away. Gradually build up a line of six jumps.

Rules for the Road

Here are some of the rules and signals you must know before riding on the road. These riders are all on the left because they live in a country, such as Australia or England, where the traffic drives on the left. If you live in a country, such as America, Germany, France, Italy or Holland, where the traffic drives on the right hand side of the road, then you must always ride on that side of the road too.

Riding on the Road

Do not ride on the road unless your pony is quiet in traffic. Keep him alert at a walk or slow trot so he will not slip or get out of control.

Turning

Signal clearly like this and in good time if you are going to turn left. Make the same signal with your right arm if you are going to turn right.

Stopping Traffic

Hold up your hand and look straight at the driver so he knows you mean him. Wait until you are sure the traffic has stopped before you cross.

I am going to stop

Wave your outside arm up and down like this from the shoulder. This tells drivers you are going to stop and asks passing traffic to slow down.

Riding in Groups

The first and last riders give signals. Ride this distance from the pony in front. Do not change pace without telling the others, or become separated from them.

"Thank You"

Thank everyone, with a nod or a smile, who is helpful. If the road is narrow and winding, go into a gateway or on to a grass verge to let traffic pass.

Riding on the Grass Verge

Ride on grass verges wherever possible, unless they are private or trimmed and mown. Never canter along a road verge. Your pony might shy into the traffic.

Leading Another Pony

Only lead another pony if you are experienced. Then have the led pony in a bridle on your inside, with his head level with your knee. This helps to control him.

Danger Ahead

Wait until the road is clear. Then ride firmly past the frightening object. Talk to your pony quietly and pat him to keep him calm. If he really plays up, get off.

Riding at Night

If possible, do not ride at night or in a fog. If you must, always wear stirrup lights which shine white in front and red behind to warn other traffic you are there.

Country Code

There are special unwritten rules for people who ride in the countryside. Always take extra care of other people's land and property. Remember you have a right to ride on roads, bridle paths and some other special areas. But all other fields, paths and woods are private. So always get permission first from the farmer or land owner. If you do this, behave sensibly and do no damage, you may be allowed to ride there again.

Starting Off

Check that your pony is well shod, that his tack is safe and that it fits properly. Always wear a hard hat, sensible clothes and plain shoes with a small heel. If you are going out riding alone, remember to tell someone where you are going and about how long you expect to be out.

Closing Gates

Always remember to close gates that you have opened, even if the field seems empty. Teach your pony to help you do this.

Keep to Field Edges

Avoid damaging crops and fields, especially in wet weather. Be careful not to disturb livestock as you ride through fields.

Riding Uphill

Lean forward a little to leave your pony's back and hind legs free to push on up the hill. Allow him to stretch his neck when making the extra effort.

Riding Downhill

Keep your pony steady and lean forward a little to leave his back and hind quarters free. This will help him keep his balance.

Where to Canter

Choose a quiet, slightly uphill path with soft ground, or the edge of a field if you can keep in control. Slow down to pass people on foot or other riders.

On a Long Trek

Stop for a rest of about half an hour. Have a head collar over the bridle so you can take it off to let him graze. Remove the saddle and give him a short drink.

The Last Mile

It is tempting to hurry home. But you should walk the last mile to bring your pony home cool and dry. Lead him if he is very tired or refuses to walk quietly.

Back Home

A stabled pony must be rubbed down or walked until dry. If your pony is kept at grass, turn him out and he will rub himself down by having a good roll.

Popular Breeds of Ponies

The many different breeds of ponies have special qualities of size, strength and speed, which have developed over hundreds of years. Almost all are tough, gentle and quick to learn. This makes them ideal for children to ride.

There are many different types of this popular breed. Most make good riding ponies, being tough, calm, sure-footed and quiet in traffic.

New Forest

Shetland

The smallest British breed at up to 1.1 metres. Shetland ponies can be any colour but black, brown and chestnut are the most usual. They are strong for their size and, if well trained, are specially good for small children to ride.

Pony of the Americas

This new breed was formed in 1956 by mating a Shetland stallion with an Appaloosa mare. The result was a very small Appaloosa which has become popular in America as a child's pony. Usually they have white coats, peppered with spots of coloured hair.

Fjord

Iceland

These quiet ponies are becoming more popular outside their native country of Norway. They are easy to spot by their dun colour with black legs and black hairs in their manes and tails. They make good steady ponies to ride and drive, being tough, easy to feed and very good natured.

These tough little ponies of under 13 hands were brought to Iceland in the 9th century. Some work as pack ponies. Others, which are ridden, learn a special pace which is half-walk, half-trot.

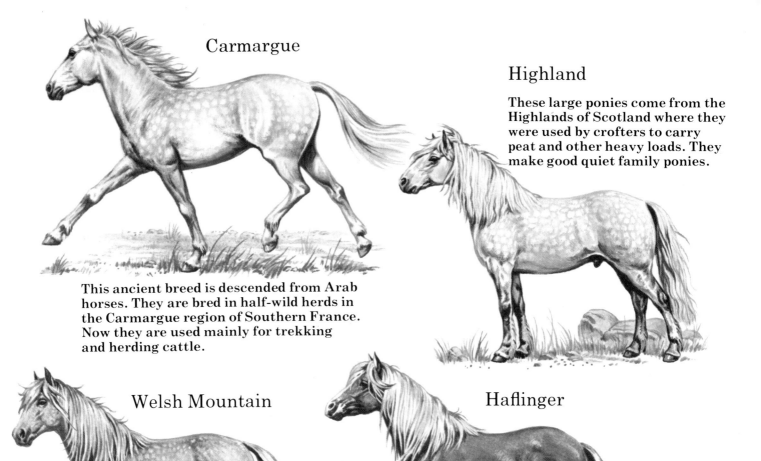

Carmargue

Highland

These large ponies come from the Highlands of Scotland where they were used by crofters to carry peat and other heavy loads. They make good quiet family ponies.

This ancient breed is descended from Arab horses. They are bred in half-wild herds in the Carmargue region of Southern France. Now they are used mainly for trekking and herding cattle.

Welsh Mountain

Haflinger

These beautiful ponies, with flowing manes and tails, have lived in Wales since Roman times. They are popular all over the world for riding, driving and breeding, being good natured, strong and nimble.

All Haflinger ponies can be traced back to one chestnut stallion called Folie, born in Austria in 1874. They are tough, sure-footed ponies and used to living in mountains. They are now popular in many countries.

Connemara

Exmoor

This breed is thought to have been produced by Arab horses, saved from wrecks of Spanish Armada ships, which bred with ponies in Ireland. Their Arab gentleness and smooth walking stride make them ideal family ponies.

These ponies with light coloured muzzles still live in half-wild herds on Exmoor. They are only about 12.3 hands high, but are sure-footed, have a smooth flat trot and are fast and good at jumping.

Telling a Pony's Age

The age of a pony or horse can be told by looking at its front teeth. There are six in the top jaw and six in the lower jaw. You can be fairly exact up to eight years old but after that it is more difficult. Then only experts can be really accurate because there are so many things to be taken into account. Look at the size and shape of a pony's front teeth to see how they change as he grows older.

A Pony's Jaw

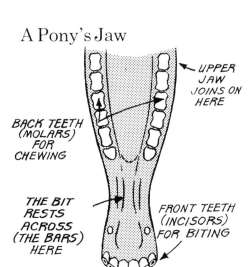

UPPER JAW JOINS ON HERE

BACK TEETH (MOLARS) FOR CHEWING

THE BIT RESTS ACROSS (THE BARS) HERE

FRONT TEETH (INCISORS) FOR BITING

This is what a pony's bottom teeth look like from above. He uses his front teeth to bite off tufts of grass and the back ones to chew it.

Two Years
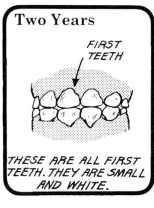
FIRST TEETH

THESE ARE ALL FIRST TEETH. THEY ARE SMALL AND WHITE.

Three Years
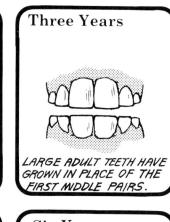
LARGE ADULT TEETH HAVE GROWN IN PLACE OF THE FIRST MIDDLE PAIRS.

Four Years

PERMANENT TEETH HAVE GROWN IN PLACE OF THE NEXT PAIRS.

Five Years
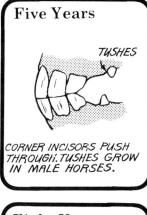
TUSHES

CORNER INCISORS PUSH THROUGH. TUSHES GROW IN MALE HORSES.

Six Years
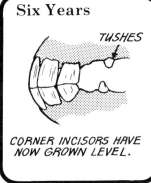
TUSHES

CORNER INCISORS HAVE NOW GROWN LEVEL.

Seven Years
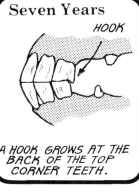
HOOK

A HOOK GROWS AT THE BACK OF THE TOP CORNER TEETH.

Eight Years

THE HOOK IS WORN AWAY. THE TEETH LOOK MORE LEVEL.

Ten Years

GROOVE

TEETH SLOPE SLIGHTLY. A GROOVE APPEARS IN CORNER TEETH.

Twenty Years
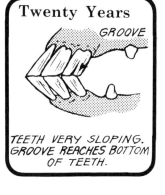
GROOVE

TEETH VERY SLOPING. GROOVE REACHES BOTTOM OF TEETH.

A Young Pony

A Fully-Grown Pony

An Old Pony

This pony is under two years old. His bones are soft and he is still growing, so his rump may be higher than his withers. He is alert and interested in everything.

A mature pony of about eight years old is in the prime of his life. He looks proud and confident, and is well-muscled and strong. Hollows over his eyes may begin to show.

This pony is nearly 30. He looks thin and bony. His muscles are slack and he may not eat well. The hollows over his eyes are deep and his movements have become stiff.

Making Your Own Jumps

You can make your own practice jumps quite easily and cheaply with a few simple things. But only use safe ones which will not hurt a pony if he hits them with his legs. Change the jumps and move them round often so that a pony does not get bored. Here are some ways to make simple jumps.

Oil Drums

The simplest way to make many kinds of jumps is by using large, empty oil drums. You can probably get them from a local garage. Stand them upright, lay them down, or use them with poles.

Poles in the Ground

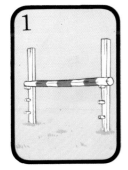 

Nail blocks of wood or pieces of a car tyre to wooden stakes to hold up poles. Ask someone to help you knock the upright stakes at least 50 cm into the ground.

Ditches

Dig a ditch about 3 metres long and 1 metre wide. Jump over it like this or with a pole across it. Line the ditch with a sheet of plastic if you want to fill it with water.

Straw Bales

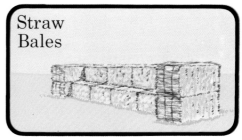

Straw bales make a very easy jump. Set up a single row of bales, end to end, or a double row with a third row on top to make a spread fence. Put some at the sides.

Car Tyres

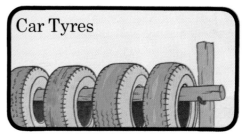

Ask your local garage for six or eight old car tyres. Hang them on a pole, like this. Make it easier by putting another pole on the ground in front of the jump.

Tree Trunks

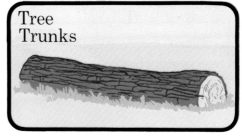

You can use anything in a field, such as a fallen tree, as a jump. Trim off any stumps of branches and saw off sharp edges which might catch a pony's feet.

Brush Fences

Nail two planks of wood to each side of upright supports, like this. Fill the gap with lots of brush twigs cut from a hedge.

Training a Young Pony

The first stage of training a young pony is to handle him and gain his confidence. This can start when he is only a few months old. He can learn to be led and obey words such as 'whoa', 'walk' and 'trot'. If he learns these early lessons well, it will help him to train and work happily with people all his life. At three years old he will be strong enough to be ridden. Training a pony for riding needs skill and experience. No two ponies are the same, and all trainers use different methods. Ponies should be trained only by a knowledgeable person as bad habits learned when young are hard to correct later. Here are some of the main stages.

Lungeing

This is used to teach young ponies obedience, and to get them fit and supple before they are ridden. It is best to start in an enclosed space. Some trainers have an assistant at first. A pony that already knows the commands will soon get the idea. A whip is used to encourage him forward and keep him out on the circle. The aim is to walk or trot the pony to the right or left, keeping his paces even and rhythmic. This is tiring, so ten minutes each way will be enough for him at first.

Parts of a Cavesson

This is a strong leather or nylon headcollar. It has three rings on a metal nosepiece to attach lungeing or side reins, and an extra throat-lash to stop it slipping.

1 Backing

This is done very gradually, so the pony is not frightened. The rider leans over his back first to get him used to the weight and sight of someone above him.

2

Then, gently and quietly, the rider is given a leg up and sits still. As the pony gets used to this he is led further each day. Then he is lunged with the rider on.

Using Side Reins

This pony is being lunged with his tack on. At this stage the trainer may decide to use side reins. They go from the side rings of the cavesson to the girth. They teach the pony to carry his head properly, to turn and bend in the direction he is going, and to balance himself. Elasticated reins are best because they have some 'give', like a rider's hands. Later when the training is more advanced they can be attached to the rings of the bit to get the pony used to pressure on the bars of his mouth.

Training for the Roads

Once he is quiet to ride, the pony should get used to traffic. At first he is taken out with others on a wide road with a grass verge if possible. When he gains confidence, he can walk in front, until finally he is ready to go alone.

Teaching a Pony to Jump

Once he trots happily over poles, he can be put over small jumps. The trainer should lunge him on a half-circle but allow him a straight approach. A pole against the side of the jump will stop the lunge rein catching or the pony running out.

Improve Your Riding—1

You will need lots of training and practice to become a really good rider. But you cannot get better on your own—your pony must get better too. Your position in the saddle, for example, will not be secure if your pony is unbalanced. So you and your pony must work together as a team if you want to learn to ride really well. The next four pages show some of the things you need to think about and practise.

Firstly, 'Impulsion'; this means the power which drives your pony forward. It has to come from his hind legs.

Secondly, 'Carriage'; this is how your pony moves and carries his weight and yours.

Thirdly, 'Suppleness'; a stiff pony will not feel nice to ride. You should do special exercises to make him supple.

All this takes a long time. You will need lots of patience and the help of a teacher.

Improve Your Position

You will be able to create impulsion in your pony only if you have a strong, balanced seat. This leaves your lower legs free to make your pony move forward energetically.

A good way to help you do this is by trotting on the lunge without holding the reins and without your feet in the stirrups. This will improve balance and leg position.

Impulsion

Your pony should feel as if he has energy stored up in his hind-quarters, ready to drive him forward at your command. This is called impulsion. It is as if his engine is at the back and your legs tell him when to use it.

A young pony, or one that has been incorrectly trained, may feel as if he is going to stop unless you keep nagging at him with your heels. This is because his hind leg muscles are not yet strong and he has not yet learned to use his hocks to push him forward.

An Untrained Pony

He carries most of his weight over his fore legs with his head low and neck stuck out. He does not use his hocks much and his hindquarters are fairly weak.

A Highly-trained Pony

With correct riding and training, a pony learns to carry more weight on his hind legs. He is lighter in front, moves more freely, and is easier to control.

Accepting the Bit

A pony is said to be 'accepting the bit' when he lets the bit rest against the sensitive sides of his mouth, without resisting or trying to avoid messages from the rider's hands. This is an important part of the training. Once he accepts the pressure of the bit, he can be taught to change pace and direction, keeping his head steady.

Some Common Faults

Above the Bit

The pony carries his head high to avoid pressure of the bit. His neck is stiff, so he is hard to control.

Overbent

The pony tucks his head in towards his chest, and pulls against the rider's hands.

Behind the Bit

Instead of obeying the rider's signals, the pony shortens his neck and 'drops' the bit.

Poking the Nose

A stiff jaw and straight neck is usually due to bad riding or a pony not using his hind legs correctly.

Carriage

Your pony will begin to look rounder and stronger as his training progresses and he becomes fitter. His hindquarters do more of the work, so he begins to carry himself well and to look more relaxed and confident.

To see if he has reached this stage, push your hands right forward for a couple of strides when you are trotting. If he is carrying himself properly, his head and neck will stay in the same position and he will keep trotting at the same speed.

Lowering Your Pony's Head

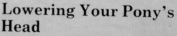
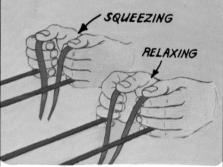

Your hands must be gentle and sensitive. Tighten or 'squeeze' your fingers on the reins. Then relax them at once, when your pony accepts the pressure and relaxes his jaw.

Raising Your Pony's Head

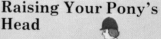

Do not try to pull his head up. Use your seat and legs to get his hind legs working harder. This will make his front or forehand lighter, and so raise his head.

Improve Your Riding—2

Suppleness

This is very important because your pony will be able to change pace and direction more easily, without getting unbalanced, if he is really supple.

He may have a stiff side and you will have to do more work in that direction to make both sides supple. These pages show some exercises for suppleness. Practise them for short periods with an instructor.

Figure-of-Eight

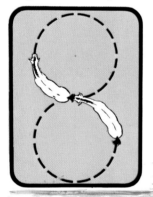

A good suppling exercise is to trot a figure-of-eight. Then your pony bends his spine first one way, then the other.

Lateral Work

When riding normally your pony's hind legs should follow the tracks of his fore legs. This is called being 'on one track'. Some of the best exercises for making your pony more supple are ones where he moves his hind legs off the track of his fore legs. This is called lateral work. These exercises will help to make your pony more supple, because he will bend his spine and body, and use his hind legs more strongly.

Advanced riders use lateral work when training young horses. It is also a good way to keep horses fit. The exercises shown below teach a pony to be obedient and so give a rider greater control.

Turn on the Forehand

Teach your pony to turn on his forehand like this. Hold your pony's head still. Tap his side so his hind legs move away from you. His front legs will go up and down on the spot.

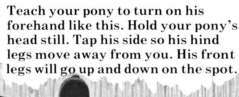
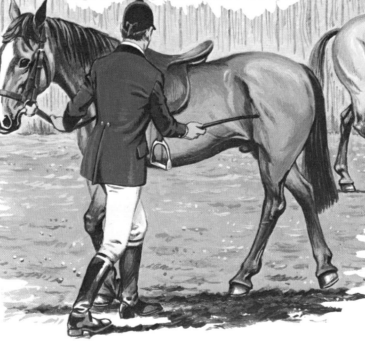

Now give him the same aids from the saddle. Your hands stop him moving forward. Now feel the right rein and use your right leg behind the girth to push his quarters over.

Sitting Correctly

You should sit in the saddle easily and with confidence, as if you and your pony are joined together. Sit with your knees and thighs close to the saddle, and your arms and lower legs relaxed. Then you can tell your pony what to do by giving him small aids. You will be able to feel with your hands and your seat how he is reacting to them.

Wrong—leaning too far forward

Wrong—stiff hollow back

Wrong—leaning too far back

Right—sitting correctly ready to give aids

70

The Half-Halt

This is an almost invisible way of getting your pony balanced and attentive before you ask him to turn or change his pace. Sit deep in the saddle and close your legs on the girth. At the same time, close your hands on the reins to stop the pony increasing his speed. The moment you feel the pony's hindquarters coming under him and the weight being taken off his fore legs, stop both your hand and leg aids on the reins and the girth.

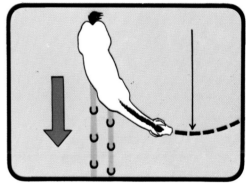

Shoulder-In

For this exercise, the pony is bent inwards from the side of the school, as if to walk in a circle. But he moves forward on a straight line. It is the only exercise when the pony's head is turned away from the direction he is going in.

This makes the pony more supple and helps the rider to get control of his pony's hindquarters. This will make it easier to stop him shying on rides.

Aids for Left Shoulder-In

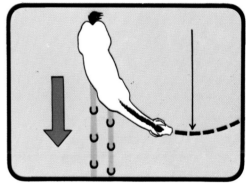

As you trot round a corner, go on giving the aids for turning, so that the pony is bent inwards. Now push him forward with your left leg.

Working Trot	Medium Trot	Collected Trot	Extended Trot

In advanced dressage, a horse has to show four different tempos of pace. They should all be at the same speed with a difference only in the length and height of step. Most work is done at working tempo. It is an active pace with regular flowing strides.	Now the horse begins to lengthen his stride. His hocks are well under him, pushing him forward with greater impulsion. Your pony should be able to show a clear difference between a working and medium trot.	This can be asked for only when the horse is very experienced, supple and well balanced. It is a slow and powerful movement with short strides. The horse carries himself higher, with raised and arched neck. The rider sits to this pace.	This is the most advanced tempo, in which the horse lengthens his stride to cover as much ground as possible. His hindquarters have to be very strong to carry the rider's weight, leaving his shoulders free to make long, straight strides.

Improve Your Jumping

Most ponies can learn to tackle successfully a course of jumps about 1 metre high—with careful training. But not every pony can become a top-class show jumper. Your pony must be at least five years old and in good condition before you start jumping. It is strenuous work and you must both be fit. Basic schooling and work over cavaletti will help his jumping muscles and make him obedient.

Start with small jumps and gradually make them bigger as your pony gains confidence. Be careful not to do too much and put him off altogether. With a few poles and supports painted in bright colours, you can make lots of different jumps. Move them round to change the distances between them and directions. This is what you will meet in the show ring. Always reward your pony with a pat and a rest when he does well.

The Jumping Position

Placing A Pony

To keep in balance with your pony during a jump you must change your position slightly. Shorten your stirrups two holes and tilt your body forward a little. Practise riding like this over small jumps, trying not to lean too far forward or letting your legs swing back.

Lungeing Over A Fence

This is very good training. It improves your balance and helps you to develop a firm position in the saddle. Hold a neck strap until you feel confident. Then practise without stirrups or reins. Try it with your eyes shut to help you feel the stride.

A good rider brings his pony up to a jump, properly balanced, and with enough impulsion to clear it. He can shorten or lengthen his pony's stride to meet the fence correctly. Before you can do this, you must be able to feel the stride and learn to judge the distance to the best take-off point. This takes quite a lot of experience. Practise counting the strides as you ride up to jump. A marker and pole, arranged like this, will help you. The pole on the ground one pace from the jump prepares the pony to take off in the correct place.

Refusing A Jump

Even a good jumper may sometimes reach a fence unbalanced and stop. Try again and he will sail over. This is nothing to worry about. But if he often refuses, you must find the reason.

The jump may be too high; the hard ground may hurt his legs or perhaps you do not ride with enough determination. Get him to clear a lower jump and reward him.

A Jumping Lane

Once your pony is fit, going down a lane of jumps will give him more confidence. It will help him to judge his own stride and think quickly. Keep up the impulsion so he does not stop in the middle. Make your own lane with a hedge on one side and a fence on the other.

The Wrong Way to Jump

Rider left behind. Weight in the wrong place.

Too far forwards, too soon. Will unbalance the pony.

Legs slipped back and up. Rider cannot give aids.

Never look down. Always ahead to the next jump.

Different Types of Show Jumps

Here are some of the jumps you will find in show rings. Different types of fences test different skills of ponies and riders. Practise at home so your pony is used to the jumps before he meets them in the ring. Study their different shapes and the way they are made. Then you can put up your own and get to know them well.

Upright

Straight up and down jumps, such as poles, planks, gates or walls, can be quite difficult for a pony, especially if there is no clear ground line.

Your pony should approach the jump with his head fairly low to judge its height and where to take off. His speed and balance of approach are very important. If it is too fast and heavy in front, he may hit the fence with his front legs or take off too soon and land on it with his hind legs.

Spread

Here a pony has to jump width as well as height. Fences such as sloping bars, shown here, triples and hogs backs, are inviting because the front part is lower than the back. A pony can get in close to make his take-off from near the gound line. The approach can be a little faster than for upright jumps to help him clear the spread.

Low spreads are useful for giving a pony confidence and encouraging him to stretch and round his back.

Parallel Jump

This is a more difficult type of spread fence because the front and back parts are the same height. A pony may find it hard to judge how wide he must jump to clear it. This fence needs a big jump from an accurate take-off position.

It may be made of poles or an oxer, which is a low hedge with higher poles on either side. High parallel poles should be used in competitions only for experienced ponies because they are so hard to jump.

Water Jump

This is a special kind of spread fence which has always been used in big events. It is now becoming more common at local shows. It sometimes causes problems because many ponies are not used to it.

Ride at a water jump at a strong canter. If you gallop, your pony may not have enough spring to clear it. He must be able to jump quite high to make the length. Easy water jumps have a pole across the middle to give them height.

Combination Jump

A jump is called a combination when two or three obstacles are placed close together. Then a pony can take only one or two strides between each jump.

A double has two jumps and a treble has three. This kind of fence is a real test of the rider's skill and the obedience of the pony. It is important to keep up enough impulsion to clear all the parts and be able to adjust the pony's stride so he meets each one correctly.

Getting Ready for a Show

Shows are great fun. You meet friends and their ponies, and can enjoy competing against them. There are so many different events that whatever type of pony you have, there will be something for you. Look in your local newspaper, or horse and pony magazines for likely shows.

Write off for schedules for different shows and then study them carefully. Do not enter for too many classes, particularly if your pony lives at grass.

Check the rules to make sure your age and your pony's height are right for the classes you want to enter.

If the entries have to be in by a certain date, send yours in good time. Jumping classes may be limited to a certain number. Unless you can hack or have your own horse box, you must arrange transport. Here are some things you can do that will help your pony to look his best on the day.

Extra Training

Give your pony regular steady exercise for some weeks before the show to get him fit. Plan a training course to teach him what he has to do in his class.

Trimming

Trim his heels, and the long whiskers under his chin with scissors and a comb. Shorten and thin his mane by pulling out the long hairs from underneath.

Cleaning Tack

Oil the leather well if it is dry. The day before the show, undo all the buckles and give it a good clean. Polish the metal parts and leave everything ready to use.

Extra Grooming

Start a few weeks before a show, unless your pony is living at grass in cold weather. Firm strokes with a body brush will tone up his muscles and make his coat shine.

Extra Feeding

Food, such as pony nuts, oats and barley will help to make your pony look good and give him energy. Try not to let him get fat on grass, as fat ponies tire quickly.

Tail Washing

Do this the day before the show. Use a mild shampoo, taking care to rinse it all out. Undo the tangles and put on a tail bandage to make his tail a neat shape.

Things to Take to a Show

Make a list of the things you may need and check you have them before you leave home.

Tack for Pony
- saddle
- bridle
- martingale
- brushing boots
- studs

Travelling Kit
- head collar
- rope
- anti-sweat rug
- knee pads

Other things
- grooming kit
- first-aid box
- haynet
- feed
- water bucket

The Morning of the Show

Leave plenty of time to get ready. Feed your pony early, then groom him. Plait his mane if you are entering a showing class or want to look very smart. This can take over an hour. When you have done this, get yourself ready. Wear jeans over your jodhpurs to keep them clean.

If you are travelling by horse box prepare your pony for the journey. Bandage his legs and tail to protect them, and put on a rug if it is cold. Put all the things you need for the day into the horse box first. Then your pony will not get upset waiting about once he is in it. Park

the horse box in a quiet spot. Lead your pony calmly in with some food. If you are hacking to the show, allow enough time to ride slowly and have a rest before your class. If you can, ask someone else to bring your things for you. If not, take as few as possible in a bag.

Arriving at the Show

Park near the ring for your classes so you can follow the programme and hear the loudspeaker without moving far from your pony. Check that he has travelled well and unload him carefully. This pony had room to turn round but ponies often have to back out of a box.

If you have hacked to the show, or cannot leave your pony in his box find a quiet, shady spot to tie him up. Avoid barbed wire fences, and do not leave him too close to a strange pony. Ask someone to keep an eye on him while you go to the secretary's tent.

Riding a Show Jumping Course

Show jumping is a very popular and well-organized sport. Make sure you know the rules before you start. The aim is not to jump the highest, but to clear the course without faults. For some competitions, neither the pony nor the rider can have won a prize before.

Others limit the rider's age or pony's height. Choose carefully, so you ride against others of about your own age and class.

If you and others jump a clear round, you will have to jump again. This is called a jump-off. It is usually over a shorter course of higher jumps. It may be 'against the clock'. This means that if two riders have the same number of faults, the faster one wins.

Enjoy your success when you win, but do not be disappointed if you lose.

Arrive Early

Collect your number and jumping order from the secretary. If you can choose your turn, make it not too near the beginning. Then you can get a few tips watching others.

Walking the Course

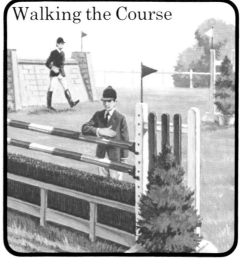

A plan of the course is pinned up at most shows. Study this, then walk the actual circuit of jumps that you will take on your pony. Note any tricky jumps or turns.

In the Collecting Ring

Go into the collecting ring a few minutes before your number will be called. Walk calmly round to keep your pony alert and warm. When you are called, walk into the arena.

At the Start

Ride round, getting your pony used to the ring while you wait for the signal to start. Check that he is cantering on the right leg. Pass through the start and off you go.

Looking Ahead

While you are taking one jump, try to think about and look ahead to the next. Remember your pony does not know the way. He depends on you to guide him.

'Well Done'

Leave the ring at a walk. Pat and make much of your pony even if you have not done well. Dismount and loosen the girth. Never punish him for a mistake made in the ring.

78

A Show Jumping Course

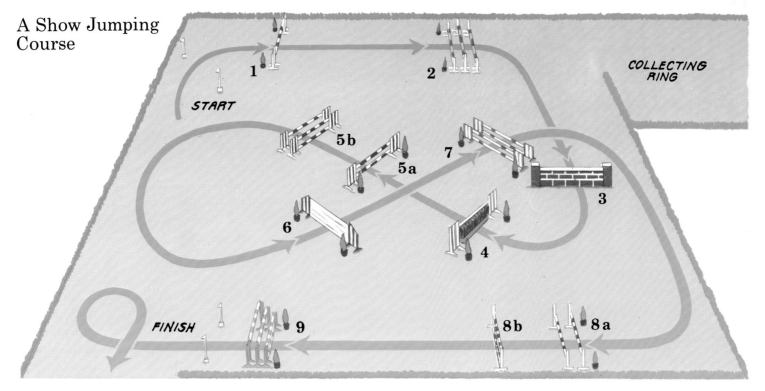

START

COLLECTING RING

1
2
5b
5a
7
3
6
4
8b
8a
9
FINISH

A junior course usually has at least seven jumps, including a combination. They are carefully set out by the course-builder to test the skill of pony and rider.

The scores for most classes are: 4 faults for a knock down, 3 for the first refusal, 6 for the second, and elimination at the third. There are 8 faults for a fall.

1. Upright of poles
2. Hog's back
3. Wall
4. Brush under white pole
5. Double (a) upright (b) spread
6. Gate
7. Parallel poles
8. Double (a) spread (b) upright
9. Triple pole

Some Rules to Remember

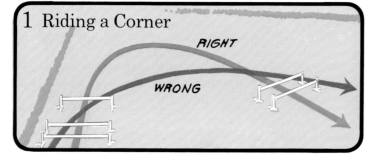

1 Riding a Corner

RIGHT

WRONG

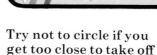

Make a wide corner, so your pony does not have to jump at an angle. Then he will have time to judge the height and adjust his stride to clear it.

2

RIGHT

WRONG

Try not to circle if you get too close to take off or lose control. This counts as a refusal. Swing back in a wide arc to get a longer run.

Refusals

If your pony refuses, give him one sharp tap with your stick and turn him back across the fence. Canter a semi-circle and bring him in again. Ride with great determination at the centre of the jump.

Falls

If either or both of you fall, quickly check that your pony is not hurt. Then remount and continue. If you fall before you complete the jump, then you must go back and jump it again.

Gymkhanas

Gymkhana events are games played on horseback. You can usually enter for these at a show on the day itself. There are different classes for all ages to give everyone a fair chance. Choose events your pony is best at. Do not enter for too many classes or your pony will get tired and be unable to do his best. Teams of riders from different Pony Clubs often play against each other at horse shows and against teams from other countries.

What Makes a Good Gymkhana Pony

Almost any pony can become good at gymkhana events. The secret lies in patient practice at home, doing everything slowly at first. Speed is important but your pony must also be obedient and quick at turning and stopping. Teach him to stop as soon as you take your feet out of the stirrups. Practise leading so he runs beside you easily. Learn to jump on and off quickly and ride with one hand. These children are practising musical sacks, racing to reach the sack first when the music stops.

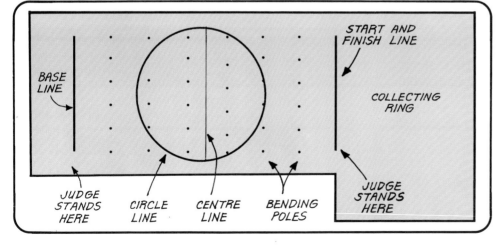

How the Arena is Set Out

The arena will be set out something like this. The start and end lines are usually drawn in white, but may just be marked by flags at each end. Games like Bending Races usually take place first. Then the poles are removed. Wait for your event in the collecting ring, leaving the exit clear for other riders to get in and out.

Some Gymkhana Rules

As for all other kinds of riding, you must wear a hard hat. One with a soft or collapsible peak, and a chin strap to stop it coming off, is best.

You may not carry a whip or wear spurs and if a pony behaves badly, it may be sent out.

A lame or unfit pony, or one under four years old, may not take part. If you drop something during a race, such as a baton, you may pick it up and carry on. But if you knock down or miss a bending pole, and do not go back, you will be eliminated.

Gymkhana Games

Here are some games that you may like to enter for. If there are lots of competitors, you may have to ride in a heat first. The winners compete in the final.

Bending Race

Race down the arena weaving in and out of your line of poles. Turn round the one at the end. Then race back to the finishing line, in and out of the poles again.

Flag Race

Pick up a flag, gallop down the field to the empty holder and stick it in. Do this one at a time with all your flags, and then race back to the finishing line.

Sack Race

Gallop from the starting line to your sack. Leap off and jump in. Push your toes well down into the corners. Hop or run to the finishing line, leading your pony.

Balloon Race

This is like a flag race except that you burst a balloon tied to a post every time you race up the arena. Make sure your pony is used to balloons and bangs beforehand.

Potato Picking Scramble

The idea is to collect as many potatoes as possible from the middle of the arena, and drop them into your bucket. You may only carry one potato at a time.

'Chase-Me-Charlie'

Riders take the jump one after the other. Anyone who knocks it down or refuses is out. It is raised after each round and the winner is the one who jumps the highest.

Obstacle Races

These sorts of races can have lots of different obstacles. You may have to run along a row of

upturned flower pots leading your pony, crawl through a tyre or under a hurdle, then run in a sack. There

is often a simple jump, a needle to thread, or a sack of straw or an egg and spoon to carry.

Pony Trekking

Pony trekking is something you can enjoy, whether you have ridden before or not. Holidays usually last a week and some centres welcome children without their parents. Write to your Tourist Board for a list of centres. Try to choose one that is approved by a horse or pony society.

You will go for a long trek each day and return to your hostel or hotel at night. A few centres arrange for trekkers to ride on, staying at different places at night. This is called post trekking.

What to Take

Take clothes for hot or cold weather with plenty of T-shirts and thick, warm sweaters. Riding or corduroy trousers are strong and comfortable. Jodhpurs may feel tight and jeans will rub your legs on a long hot day. Take lace-up shoes or riding boots to ride in, and a pair of wellingtons for stable work on wet days.

Ready to Set Off

Be prepared for any sort of weather. Take warm, comfortable clothes because it can be cold in the hills even in mid-summer. Your pony must be comfortable too. Check that he has no girth or saddle sores. His shoes must fit tightly with no nails sticking up. Never set off on a lame pony or one that seems to be very thin.

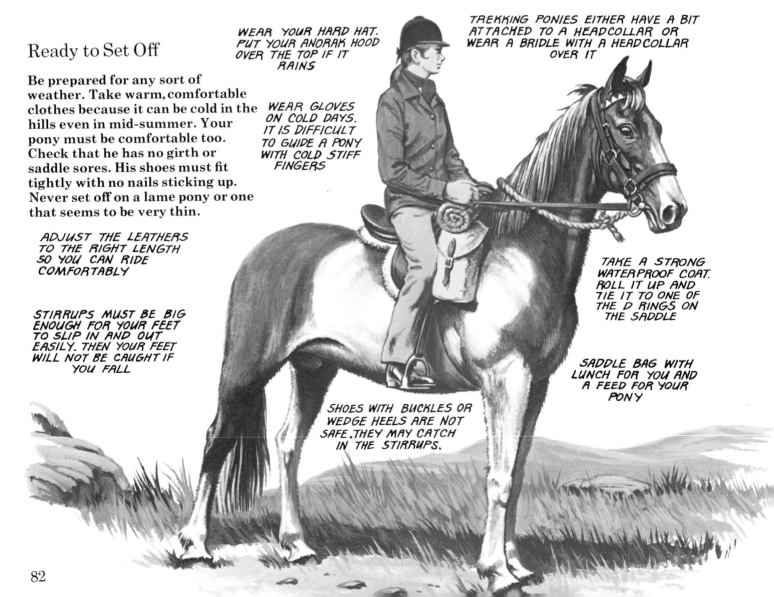

WEAR YOUR HARD HAT. PUT YOUR ANORAK HOOD OVER THE TOP IF IT RAINS

WEAR GLOVES ON COLD DAYS. IT IS DIFFICULT TO GUIDE A PONY WITH COLD STIFF FINGERS

TREKKING PONIES EITHER HAVE A BIT ATTACHED TO A HEADCOLLAR OR WEAR A BRIDLE WITH A HEADCOLLAR OVER IT

ADJUST THE LEATHERS TO THE RIGHT LENGTH SO YOU CAN RIDE COMFORTABLY

STIRRUPS MUST BE BIG ENOUGH FOR YOUR FEET TO SLIP IN AND OUT EASILY. THEN YOUR FEET WILL NOT BE CAUGHT IF YOU FALL

TAKE A STRONG WATERPROOF COAT. ROLL IT UP AND TIE IT TO ONE OF THE D RINGS ON THE SADDLE

SADDLE BAG WITH LUNCH FOR YOU AND A FEED FOR YOUR PONY

SHOES WITH BUCKLES OR WEDGE HEELS ARE NOT SAFE. THEY MAY CATCH IN THE STIRRUPS.

When You Arrive

The first day will be spent settling in and getting to know the pony that you will be riding. Perhaps you may have a short ride on the first afternoon. Listen carefully to all instructions and follow the stable routine.

Grooming and Tacking Up

At some centres you are expected to do this, while at others you can help if you like. Groom before setting out in the morning. Remove mud and dried sweat with a dandy brush and pick out his feet before putting on the saddle and bridle.

Out in the Country

Pony treks usually move at a walk because of the kind of country and long distances. There is always a leader who knows the ponies and the country-side, and who will look after younger riders and those who have not ridden before. Keep in line or you might upset someone else's pony. You may have to get off and walk in very steep places.

Resting

There is usually a rest of about an hour for you and your pony. Either take off the saddle and set it down carefully or leave it on with the girth loosened. Take off the bridle and give your pony a drink. Then you can tie him up in the shade to graze while you have your picnic.

Horse Trials

These competitions test the all-round training and fitness of ponies and their riders. There are three parts. They are Dressage, Cross-Country and Show Jumping. The most advanced events, such as Badminton in England, Boekelo in Holland and Luhmühlen in Germany, last for three days with one part on each day.

Some Horse Trials have a shorter cross-country part and last only two days. For less experienced horses and ponies there are One-Day Events too. These have a simple dressage test, a short cross-country course and, lastly, show jumping. There are also some special events which have just dressage and show jumping.

There are lots of different grades of Horse Trials, so enter simple ones for novice ponies to begin with. Penalty points are given for mistakes and for taking longer than the time allowed. The winner is the one with the lowest score. Both you and your pony must be very fit. He will need extra energy food and a gradual training programme.

1 Dressage

This is a test to see how well trained and obedient your pony is. Advanced horses are asked to carry out very difficult movements, but tests for ponies are usually quite simple. Each rider has to perform the test in an arena. Learn and practise the movements you will have to do for 10–20 minutes each day. Vary the order you do them in or your pony will remember them and change pace or direction before you you ask him to. Concentrate on anything your pony finds difficult.

2 Cross-Country

This is the most exciting part of a horse trial. The course for big international events may be up to $7\frac{1}{2}$ km long with about 36 solid fences to be jumped. When you first start, enter for small local events where the course will probably be only about $1\frac{1}{2}$ km long with perhaps eight jumps.

All the obstacles in this part are the sort you might have to jump out on a ride. They are usually quite solid and do not knock down. Each jump will be marked with flags. Always walk the course before the competition begins. Then you will know how to help your pony jump each obstacle.

Feeder

There is a feed trough or hay rick in most courses. Look ahead and ride with determination or your pony may stop to look at it.

Do not go too fast. This jump has no ground line. Help your pony by keeping him balanced and telling him when to take off.

Tree trunk

You will have jumped these often on rides. If there are branches sticking out, choose a clear part to jump and guide your pony firmly.

Water Jump

You may have to jump into or over water. Practise doing both out on rides, so your pony will know what to do.

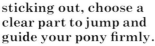

Bank

Jump on to and then immediately off a bank. Tell your pony to jump off or he may hesitate and stay on top.

In-and-Out

There is usually a sheep pen. Jump in one side and out the other. Choose the easiest way for your pony.

3 Show Jumping

Each competitor must jump one round of a show jumping course as the last part of a horse trial. This will show if your pony is still fit and obedient after galloping across country. There are usually about eight jumps. They are not high and the course is straightforward with no difficult turns. The marking is different from ordinary show jumping. You get 5 penalties for a knock-down or a first refusal, 10 for a second refusal and you are eliminated for the third. A fall costs 15 penalties.

Long-Distance Rides

Long-distance rides are tests of fitness and endurance for horses and their riders. They are popular in many countries. Some famous rides of up to 160 km are the Tevis Cup in America, the Quilty in Australia and the Golden Horseshoe in England. As well as these, there are lots of shorter ones, up to 25 km, which you and your pony can take part in. Arab horses are very successful at this sort of event. It needs a lot of skill and careful training for many weeks to get your pony really fit enough to take part in these sorts of events.

Water

There are not actual jumps on the route but you will meet all sorts of natural obstacles, like steep banks, rivers and streams. You can let your pony drink a few mouthfuls, but be careful he does not roll.

Young Riders

Pony Clubs sometimes organize rides for young riders. You can also arrange your own quite easily but check your plans with an experienced adult.

Checking the Route

Study your map carefully before the ride, to learn the symbols and get to know the area. Carry your map and route notes in a light bag on your shoulder.

Checkpoints

At special points along the route you may have to take a short rest. Your time of arrival will be noted. A vet will check your pony to see that he is still fit and sound.

Hunter Trials

These cross-country events were first started by hunts to train and get horses fit for hunting. They have now become a popular sport in many countries.

The courses are usually run over farm land, and the jumps are mainly natural obstacles. There are special courses for ponies and young riders.

Hunter trials are not races. Each competitor sets out in turn. The object is to finish the course without a refusal or a fall at a good hunting pace.

At the Start

Be ready in good time, having walked and learned the course. Exercise your pony so he is alert but not over excited. This is called 'working in'. When your number is called, check your girth, then walk towards the start.

Cross-Country Team Events

This is the newest horse sport. It started in England where it is quickly becoming very popular. Local hunts often organize events for teams of four or five riders who set out together to jump a fairly big cross-country course. The distance varies between $1\frac{1}{2}$ and $5\frac{1}{2}$ km. The team which gets the first three of its four riders home in the shortest time is the winner. There are no faults or penalty points because mistakes cost time. The members of each team plan how to complete the course. Sometimes the best horse gives a lead to the others.

Lameness

Lameness is one problem you will probably meet at some time if you look after a pony. Pain or stiffness in any of his legs will make him lame.

There are lots of different causes, and your pony cannot tell you what is the matter. So you have to look for clues to find the trouble.

These pages show you how to do this. But you must get your vet to examine the pony as well. He will decide what treatment is needed.

1 Which Leg is Lame?

Watch him trot towards you on a loose rein. If one front leg is lame, he will nod his head down as his good leg touches the ground. He takes a shorter stride with the lame leg to keep weight off it.

2

Now have him trotted away from you. If he is lame in one hind leg, you should be able to see him drop his hip on the good side. He does this to try and take the weight off the leg that hurts.

3

As he trots, he will put his lame leg down carefully to avoid pain. If the toe hits the ground first, the trouble is probably in the back of the leg. If he rests on the heel, it may be in the front.

Some Common Leg Injuries

Most ponies are strong and, if well looked-after, do not often go lame. These pictures show some of the problems which you may be able to detect by examining and feeling your pony's legs.

Lameness may be caused by a knock or the constant jarring of his legs on hard ground. A pony whose legs are not well built to act as shock absorbers is more likely to suffer from this. Examine the lame leg carefully, starting at the foot. Feel for swellings, tenderness or heat.

Even the best cared-for ponies can go lame. But if you ride sensibly and adjust your speed to the type of ground you are riding on, injuries are much less likely.

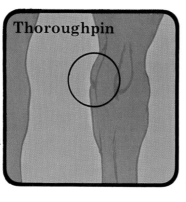

Thoroughpin

A swelling of joint fluid either side of the hock. Not painful.

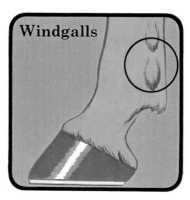

Windgalls

Little puffy swellings round the fetlock caused by work on hard ground.

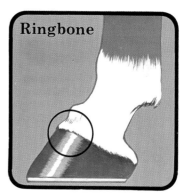

Ringbone

Extra growth of bone between the coronet and fetlock. Call the vet.

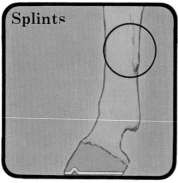

Splints

Small bony lumps made by jarring. Often only cause lameness when forming.

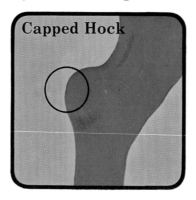

Capped Hock

An ugly lump caused by a knock or bang on the leg. Not painful.

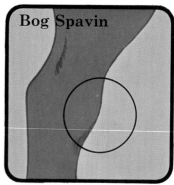

Bog Spavin

Puffy swelling caused by strain. Only serious if the swelling gets hot.

Muscle Injuries and Sprains

Tendons are strips of fibre which join muscles to bones. Ligaments join one bone to another. When a horse or pony gallops, or lands after a jump, the front tendons particularly take a lot of strain. If you make your pony do these things when he is tired or unfit, or if he lands awkwardly, he may tear tendons or ligaments,

Parts of a Pony's Foreleg

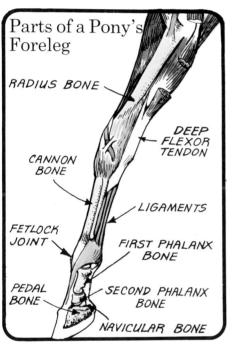

RADIUS BONE

DEEP FLEXOR TENDON

CANNON BONE

LIGAMENTS

FETLOCK JOINT

FIRST PHALANX BONE

PEDAL BONE

SECOND PHALANX BONE

NAVICULAR BONE

Remedies

If the area is infected, put on a poultice to draw out the pus. Hose knocks with cold water. Always rest your pony, even if the injury is only slight.

Foot Problems

Corns

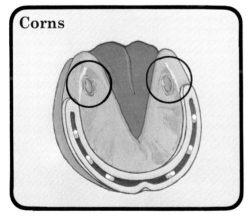

These are caused by bruising on the pony's foot, just behind the heel of the shoe. They can be caused by sharp stones, badly-fitting shoes or lack of care.

Sand Cracks

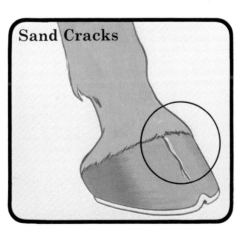

A knock or injury on the coronet damages the hoof and can cause a crack to develop. Call a vet. Grass cracks from the bottom of the foot are less serious.

Navicular

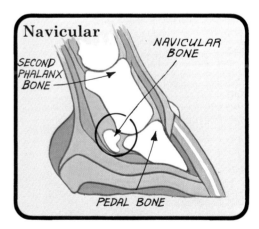

NAVICULAR BONE

SECOND PHALANX BONE

PEDAL BONE

A serious disease of the navicular bone causes permanent lameness in the front feet. There is no cure. But the pain can be relieved by cutting the nerves to the area.

More About Tack

These two pages show you some of the tack you will see on horses and ponies. Choosing and fitting the right tack should be done carefully. Most ponies are happiest in a plain snaffle bridle but some are easier to control in a special bit or noseband. Ask an experienced person for advice if you think your pony needs any kind of special bit or bridle.

Bridles

There are three main types of bridle: Single, Double and Bitless. Single bridles are the most common. The term includes all bridles that have one bit with one pair of reins. A double bridle has two bits with two pairs of reins.

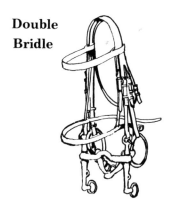

Double Bridle

Double Bridle This has an extra headpiece for the second bit. The first bit, called a Bridoon, is a small jointed snaffle, and the second bit, called a Weymouth, is a curb. It has a straight mouthpiece and long 'cheek' or side pieces. The reins are attached to rings at the bottom. A curb chain lies in the chin groove and presses against it when the lower reins are used.

Bitless Bridle

Bitless Bridle The Hackamore type is most common. The reins are attached to long cheek pieces which act like a lever on the special noseband. They press against the top and back of the nose, giving the rider control.

Dropped Noseband

Dropped Noseband This is fitted lower than a plain one and fastened at the back below the bit, in the chin groove. It stops the pony opening his mouth to escape the action of the bit.

Grakle Noseband

Grakle Noseband This has two straps that cross over on the nose and fasten behind it. It has the action of a dropped noseband and a plain one at the same time.

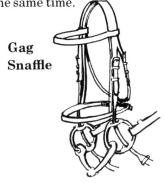

Gag Snaffle

Gag Snaffle This is a very strong type of bridle. The bit has big rings and the cheek straps run through holes in them to join directly on to the reins, giving a sharp upward action on the mouth. A second set of reins buckled on to the rings should be used as well.

Bits

There are many different types of bits for riding and driving. The gentlest one a rider can keep control with is best. Strong-action bits can make a horse's mouth hard.

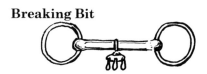

Breaking Bit

Breaking Bit is especially for getting young horses used to having a bit in their mouths. It has 'keys' in the middle to encourage the horse to play with the bit and accept it.

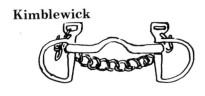

Kimblewick

Kimblewick has a straight mouthpiece with a 'port' for the tongue and 'D' shaped rings with a curb chain.

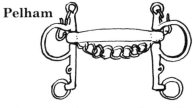

Pelham

Pelham has the two actions of a double bridle, with two sets of reins, but only one bit. The top reins have a snaffle action and the bottom ones have a lever action on the curb chain.

Liverpool Bit

Liverpool Bit is the most common driving bit. The reins can be used on the large rings or slotted through slits in the cheeks to give a curb action.

90

Martingales

These are put on to keep a horse's head down by force. They are often used when a horse may become excited and throw his head up, such as when jumping. Martingales should not be used for schooling, dressage or showing as they only draw attention to a fault in training. They can even encourage horses to hold their heads too high as many will 'lean' on martingales and throw up their heads when they are taken off, because they miss them. There are several types of martingale but the main ones are called Standing and Running.

Standing Martingale

Standing Martingale It has a leather strap looped round the girth between the front legs and attached to the back of a plain noseband. It runs through a neck strap to keep it in place.

Running Martingale

Running Martingale This is similar to the Standing one except the strap divides into two with a ring at each end. The reins are threaded through the rings so that the downward action is on the bars of the mouth.

Saddles

There are many types of saddles for different horses and horse sports. For ordinary, everyday riding, most people use a general or all-purpose saddle. There are special saddles for show jumping.

Racing Saddle

Racing Saddle This is a small pad-like saddle that is very light. Some weigh only a few hundred grammes. They have a long seat and short, forward flaps so that the jockey can ride with short stirrups. An extra elastic girth goes right round the horse's tummy and over the saddle.

Dressage Saddle

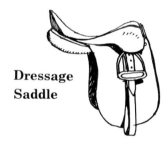

Dressage Saddle It is short in the seat but has long, straight side flaps so that the rider can have long stirrups, keeping his legs as close to the horse's sides as possible. The girth is fastened to long straps below the flaps so that the buckles are out of the way.

Side Saddle

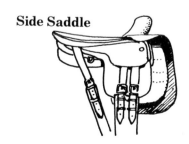

Side Saddle This is an old-fashioned lady's saddle which was designed so that the rider could wear a skirt, and ride with both legs on the same side. It has a large, flat seat with a flap and one stirrup on the near side only. The rider rests her right leg on a false pommel.

Boots

Horses often wear boots to protect their legs when they are jumping or galloping. The most common injuries are caused by brushing and over-reaching.

Brushing Boots

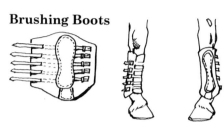

Brushing Boots guard against knocks from the opposite leg. They have a leather panel which covers the inside cannon bone and fetlock area. Four or five straps keep it firmly in place.

Yorkshire Boots

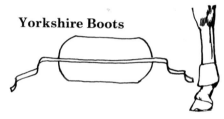

Yorkshire Boots are used to protect the hind fetlocks from brushing. A boot is an oval of thick felt with a tape sewn along it. It is tied just above the fetlock with the top folded over to give a double thickness.

Over-Reach Boots

Over-Reach Boots prevent injury to its heel if the horse over-steps himself. It looks like a rubber flower-pot and is stretched on over the hoof.

Tendon Boots

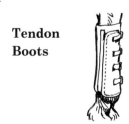

Tendon Boots also prevent an over-reach injury but are put on further up the leg. It is like a brushing boot but the padded panel fits over the back of the leg, guarding the tendons.

Horse Words and Expressions

Types of Horses and Ponies

Brood Mare—an adult female horse kept for breeding.

Cob—a stocky horse with a thick body and short, strong legs. Not higher than 15.3 hands.

Colt—a male foal up to three years old.

Dam—the mother of a horse.

Draught Horse—a type of heavy horse used for pulling heavy loads.

Filly—a female foal up to three years old.

Gelding—a neutered male horse.

Hack—a light riding horse, usually a thoroughbred.

Hackney—a light-boned horse, which steps high, used in harness.

Hackney

Hinny—the offspring of a male horse and a female donkey.

Hunter—a type of large, strong horse, not a breed but often partly thorough-bred, which can gallop and jump across country.

Jack-ass—a male donkey.

Jenny—a female donkey.

Mule—the offspring of a male donkey and a female horse.

Sire—the father of a horse.

Stallion—a male horse over three years old, usually kept only for breeding.

Yearling—a colt or filly between one and two years old.

Horse Looks and Movements

Brushing—the horse knocks the inside of one leg with the opposite leg.

Coffin head—a large, ugly head.

Cow-hocked—the points of the hock joints turn inwards.

Dished face—a horse's face which curves inwards. This is a feature of Arab horses.

Ewe-neck—a horse's neck which is longer underneath than on top. The horse carries his head awkwardly high.

Forging—when a horse hits the underneath of the toe of a front shoe with the toe of a hind shoe.

Over-reaching—when a horse hits the lower part of his front legs with a hind toe, often causing serious damage.

Parrot-mouth—when a horse's teeth in his upper jaw overlap those in his lower jaw, instead of meeting. This can stop him from eating grass.

Pigeon-toed—when a horse's fore legs are wide at the knees and the front hooves turn inwards.

Roach back—a round back caused by a bad spine.

Roman nose—a horse's face which curves outwards.

Sickle-hocked—a horse's hocks which are weak and bend outwards.

Sway or hollow back—a back that looks very dipped.

Sway or hollow back

Well-sprung ribs—a horse with a big, rounded rib-cage, giving plenty of room for heart and lungs.

People Who Work with Horses

Apprentice—a young person training for a career with horses.

Dealer—a person who buys and sells horses as a business.

Farrier or blacksmith—a person who shoes horses.

Groom—a person who looks after horses and may exercise them.

Huntsman—the person in charge of hounds. It could be the Master of Foxhounds or someone specially employed as a huntsman.

Huntsman

Instructor—a person who teaches riding.

Knacker—a person who slaughters horses for their meat.

Master of Foxhounds (M.F.H)—the person in charge of a pack of hounds.

Trainer—a person who advises on the preparation of horses and riders for all kinds of competitions.

Veterinary Surgeon—a person qualified to look after the health of animals. Some specialize in horses.

Whipper-in—a person who helps the Huntsman look after the hounds while out hunting and in the kennels.

Horse Words

Aged—a general term for horses over eight years old.

Bang tail—a tail cut square across the bottom, usually just below a horse's hocks.

Blanket clip—a coat clipped only on the head, neck, shoulders, tummy and lower quarters.

Broken wind—a permanent condition where the lungs are partly damaged, and breathing is difficult. The horse has a hollow cough. He should be fed damp food and should be worked only lightly.

Clipping—all or part of a horse's winter coat is clipped short. This stops him from getting too hot when working and so losing weight or catching cold because of standing about in a heavy, wet coat.

Dumping—a toe shortened by too much rasping or filing.

Eel-stripe—the dark line along the spine of a dun-coloured horse.

Feather—the hair growing at the back of the legs.

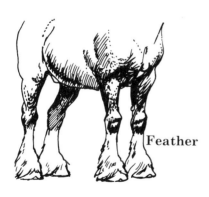

Feather

Full clip—all the winter coat is clipped short.

Green—a young, inexperienced horse.

Hard or **Iron Mouth**—when the bars of a horse's mouth have become so hard, he does not feel the pressure of the bit. Caused through rough handling or a harsh bit.

Hogged mane—a mane that is completely clipped off.

Hunter clip—all the coat is clipped short except for the legs and saddle patch.

Hunter clip

Pulled mane—a mane that is kept thin and short by pulling out hairs from underneath.

Pulled tail—the long hairs on either side of the dock are pulled out to make a tail look thin at the top.

Quartering—a way of grooming a rugged-up horse quickly in the morning. Each forehand and quarter is brushed in turn by throwing back that part of the rug. This stops a horse getting cold.

Sound—a horse that has no defects or lameness.

Star gazer—a horse which holds his head up so high that he cannot see where he is going. This is usually to avoid a painful bit.

Strapping—a very thorough grooming, usually done in the evening. Much of it is done with a body brush and muscles are toned up with a wisp.

Studs—small metal pegs which are screwed into specially-made holes in horse shoes. They stop a horse slipping on soft ground when jumping and when making a sharp turn.

Sweet itch—a horse rubs himself round his main and tail until they are very sore. This is caused by a fly which bites on warm evenings.

Switch tail—a tail is thinned at the sides so it ends in a point.

Trace clip—a coat clipped short under the neck, shoulders, tummy and quarters.

Wall eye—an eye which looks pink or blue instead of brown. This does not usually affect a horse's sight.

Bad Habits

Bucking—when a horse kicks out with both hind legs, usually in high spirits.

Bolting—when a horse gets the bit between his teeth and gallops away out of control. Usually due to bad riding.

Crib-biting—when a horse holds the edge of any surface between his teeth and sucks in air.

Crib-biting

Daisy-cutting—when a horse walks or trots without lifting its feet very high.

Dishing—when a horse swings its feet outwards when moving forwards.

Kicking—a horse's most usual way of defending himself. A kicker may have been ill-treated or just guarding his food.

Napping—when a horse refuses to go where the rider asks, often moving backwards instead. This can be cured with patience.

Nipping—when a horse snatches at a person's hand or clothes, often because he expects a titbit.

Weaving—when a stabled horse leans over a door and swings his head from side to side. Often caused by boredom, it is copied by other horses.

Wind-sucking—when a horse sucks in air and swallows it with a gulping noise. It can harm his lungs.

Index

Some Useful Addresses

Association of British Riding Schools,
Chesham House,
56 Green End Road,
Sawtry,
Huntingdon PE17 5OY.

Australian Pony Club Council,
Royal National Agricultural and
  Industrial Association of
  Queensland,
Exhibition grounds,
Gregory Terrace,
Fortitude Valley,
Brisbane 4006.

British Driving Society,
10 Marley Avenue,
New Milton,
Hants.

British Field Sports Society,
26 Caxton Street,
London S.W.1.

British Show Pony Society,
Smale Farm,
Wisborough Green,
Billinghurst,
Sussex RH14 0AU.

British Veterinary Association,
7 Mansfield Street,
Portland Place,
London W.1.

Canadian Pony Club Advisory Board,
Mrs R. W. L. Laidlaw,
29 Country Lane,
Willowdale,
Ontario M2L 1E1.

The Endurance Horse & Pony Society, (Long-distance rides)
Hyland Arabian Farm,
Bagnum Lane,
Crow,
Nr Ringwood, Hants.

National Pony Society,
Stoke Lodge,
85 Cliddesden Road,
Basingstoke,
Hants RG21 3HA.

New Zealand Pony Clubs Association,
Mrs F. H. Bond,
Lockwood,
RD5 Palmerston North,
North Island.

Ponies of Britain,
Brookside Farm,
Ascot,
Berkshire.

The Pony Club,
British Horse Society,
British Show Jumping Association,
The National Equestrian Centre,
Kenilworth,
Warwickshire CV8 2LR.

Photographs: p.12/13 E.D. Lacey; p.14/15 E.D. Lacey; p.16/17 Bob Langrish; p.10 Whitbread & Co. Ltd; p.11 United States Travel Service; p.18 (top) Bob Langrish, (lower) Werner Ernst; p.19 (top left) van der Slikke, (top right) Bob Langrish, (lower left) Bob Langrish, (lower right) E.D. Lacey; p.20/21 E.D. Lacey; p.22 (top) Bob Langrish, (lower left) Bob Langrish, (lower right) Peter Roberts; p.23 (top left, right) Jim Meads, (lower) Peter Roberts; p.24/25 Fiona Vigors Ltd; p.26 Colorlabs International; p.27 (top) Racing Information Bureau, (lower) Wallis Photographers; p.28/29 Film-und Lichtbildstelle des Bundesministeriums fur Land-und Forstwirtschaft, Wien.

PRINTED IN BELGIUM BY
proost
INTERNATIONAL BOOK PRODUCTION